Core Themes in Social Work

Power, Poverty, Politics and Values

Core Themes in Social Work

Power, Poverty, Politics and Values

Martin Sheedy

Open University Press

Open University Press
McGraw-Hill Education
McGraw-Hill House
Shoppenhangers Road
Maidenhead
Berkshire
England
SL6 2QL

email: enquiries@openup.co.uk
world wide web: www.openup.co.uk

and Two Penn Plaza, New York, NY 10121-2289, USA

First published 2013

A catalogue record of this book is available from the British Library

ISBN-13: 9780335244553 (pb)
ISBN-10: 0335244556 (pb)
e-ISBN: 9780335244560

Library of Congress Cataloging-in-Publication Data
CIP data has been applied for

Typeset by Aptara Inc., India
Printed in the UK by Bell and Bain Ltd, Glasgow.

Praise for this book

"This book sheds a very bright light on poverty as a central experience of the people social workers work with. Research and theories of power, politics and values are thoroughly discussed and provide the basis for a sustained commitment to social justice. The book is a supportive read as it skilfully appreciates the personal challenges that critical and assertive practice entails. It is a book for students, professionals and service leads to keep, re-read and savour."

Dr Tillie Curran, Senior Lecturer in Social Work,
University of the West of England, UK

"By identifying power, poverty, politics and values as core themes in social work, this text offers us a refreshing perspective which will challenge students and practitioners alike to re-evaluate their practice in the light of its wider social, political and philosophical contexts.

Through an exploration of issues of power and an interrogation of the real meaning of social work ethics and values, Sheedy motivates and encourages us to reflect on our practice and to ensure that it is truly person-centred."

Dr Sue Taplin, University of Nottingham, UK

"This book offers a concise and coherent discussion of what should be core themes in thoughtful and careful social work practice. It offers a journey towards rethinking and embracing effective critical practice, which engages with human rights and social justice as much as with empowerment and with individual and interpersonal change.

Occasional student accounts, coupled with use of key points and questions for discussion make for accessibility. The book synthesises, summarises and critiques ideas about how to understand and resolve social issues, enabling readers to question how they might work creatively alongside service users. It is a book which invites reflection on policy and practice."

Professor Michael Preston-Shoot, Dean, Faculty of Health and Social Sciences,
University of Bedfordshire, UK

"This excellent text is essential reading for all social workers and students, and a key resource for academics. It highlights – with concern and conviction – the importance of developing an effective critical practice that 'challenges, enhances and broadens the task of conventional social work' in ways that have 'the potential to improve outcomes for service users'. It calls for a

*social work practice based on an understanding of the issues of power, poli-
tics and ideology – and the values and 'world view' held by the worker – linked
with concerns raised by the people that social workers regularly encounter
and work with.*

*The issues of 'poverty and disadvantage' and their structural causes
run throughout this text – issues that have been too long neglected in social
work. In this text, Martin Sheedy corrects that neglect by outlining in some
detail the impact of poverty on people's lives and life chances whilst at the
same time describing how critical practice can be used by social workers to
promote social justice and empowerment practices."*

*Dr Pamela Trevithick, Visiting Professor in Social Work,
Buckinghamshire New University, UK*

Contents

Acknowledgements

I would like to thank the commissioning editors at Open University Press and McGraw-Hill Education, Alex Clabburn and Katherine Hartle, who have taken the time to read each draft chapter and give me clear feedback and advice. Thanks also to everyone who has influenced my thinking in writing this book.

1 A positive direction

Coming new to social work either as a student or a practitioner entering their first professional role brings with it a feeling of anxiety and an acute sense of responsibility. Apart from recognizing the complex and difficult circumstances in which social work operates, the student and worker alike might fear that they are lacking in the knowledge and understanding required for the professional arena they are entering, or experience a sense of being less knowledgeable and skilled than their peers. More experienced practitioners, on the other hand, may have difficulty finding the space to 'step outside' what they are doing and question practice in a manner which moves beyond complaint about the organizational and managerial impact on the immediate situation. This book aims to help the student and practitioner, at whatever stage in their career, to channel these anxieties into a process of locating or re-locating themselves in the arena of effective critical practice by exploring core themes central to how we think about and carry out the professional role of social worker.

To effectively apply knowledge through skills in practice it is important to fully appreciate the relationship between how the worker thinks about the world, what they do as social workers and the wider social, political and philosophical contexts in which practice occurs. Healy (2005: 2) has pointed to the lack of consideration given to 'how we might understand and respond to our practice environment, especially the philosophies and ideas underpinning our institutional contexts'. The pressure to become focused on the detail of method, policy, procedure, skills and law can often stifle opportunity for greater understanding from the beginning for the student and deter the practitioner from constructive critical reflection. A more serious danger is that it can result in acquiescence in oppressive practices.

This book aims to give students and practitioners a positive direction and motivate them to pursue a form of practice that challenges, enhances and broadens the task of conventional social work and has the potential to improve outcomes for service users. The content concerns the current, but enduring, contextual themes of social work including values, power, politics and ideology, which will contribute to the reader developing or rekindling a critical faculty with which they can better explore the detail of areas they are studying or practising in, and more fully contemplate the form of practice they intend to adopt. The book may also be used as a reference for students throughout their studies and for practitioners in the course of their work as the debate and discussion involved remain relevant to the process of reflection and refreshment at all points in the reader's career.

In engaging in these important debates on the thematic context of practice the reader will be guided towards a critical practice based on the development of a frame of thinking which will facilitate the worker in navigating a way through the complexity of the professional task. The reader will be challenged to identify or establish their own 'world view' through a knowledge and understanding of the ideological, philosophical and political options available in studying people in society. This will raise questions of the nature and content of an appropriate 'value base' for practice and bring into relief the significance of 'power' in the social worker/service user relationship. These themes will be brought together in exploring who social workers work with, leading to the core issue of 'poverty and disadvantage' across the various social divisions. Arising from this will be a recognition and understanding of the relevance of 'social sciences' to social work specifically linking the personal, the social and the political, culminating in the reader examining the nature of 'effective practice' and the qualities and characteristics of an 'effective practitioner'.

When I entered social work in the mid-1970s as part of a wider policy of graduate recruitment to the profession, there was a sense among many of us that through social work we had an opportunity to change our society towards greater equality, a redistribution of power and resources and a more economically and socially just world. This was a significant part of our vocational motivation and we recognized that there was a history of radical anti-individualism in social work. We were not so naive as to fail to realize that social work in itself was not necessarily a vehicle for such change and could just as effectively be used as a mechanism for state control. A great many changes have occurred in the decades since which have conspired to make the challenge even greater. We have had 'Thatcherism' and 'New Right' thinking in Britain both of which placed a highly popular emphasis on the individual and not the state as the source of human well-being and wealth creation through the operation of the free market unfettered by state ownership and responsibility. The ending of 'Eastern Bloc Communism' with the break up of the Soviet Union, the removal of the Berlin Wall and the end of the Cold War saw the removal of a political barrier, which heralded a marked shift towards a globalized economy based on capitalism with the growth of multi-national corporations with the virtually unrestricted movement of capital worldwide. This change has been accelerated by the 'Communication Revolution' with the World Wide Web and mobile phone technology.

These political, social and economic changes have transformed the discourse on society to the extent that there is a generally held belief, promoted by the major institutions of western society, that liberal democracy is the only valid form of government and capitalism the only viable economic system. The philosopher Francis Fukuyama (1992) highlights this process suggesting we may have reached the end of ideological evolution. Domestically political parties no longer contest each other on the basis of the relative merits of 'collectivist' and 'individualist' ideologies but in the struggle to take command of the 'middle ground'. This is exemplified by the emergence of 'New Labour' in the late 1990s, with the 'New' symbolizing its success in severing its links with socialism which once distinguished it from 'right wing' thinking embodied in conservative politics. One concern arising from these changes is that the political and ideological context of professional activity in the public sector, such as social work, is often discarded as irrelevant or worse never acknowledged from the outset. This is noticeable in the number of recruits to the social work courses I have taught on who claim no interest in or knowledge of politics and express surprise that social work might be a political activity. For the teacher of social work this presents a significant challenge.

Chris Jones and Tony Novak (1999) alert us to the fact that in the modern world of globalized capitalism social work operates in a context where the received wisdom, often promulgated by politicians, is that we have to live in the world as it is, not as we might like it to be. If previous generations had accepted such a position then the forces for change which have resisted oppression and discrimination in its various forms would not have existed. In the modern world social work still has a unique place in society through its close relationship with the poor and disadvantaged and its location, either directly or indirectly, within the state machinery. From this position it has the potential, through its practice with service users and communities and within its organizational structures, to highlight and challenge social injustice, inequality and oppression arising as direct outcomes of the economic and social systems which currently dominate. It is, of course, equally possible that from the same position, social work can also be the conduit for the implementation of oppressive policies and practices. Social work's ambivalent relationship with poverty is a case in point: much of the intervention in this sphere has historically been based on lack of money and resources being seen as the presenting problem, masking the real problem of personal, emotional and psychological deficiency. Intervention methods, in large part, are consequently designed to address the latter. This tension between focusing change on the individual or family as opposed to challenging social and economic forces is even more salient today given the prevalence of the claimed ideological and political consensus. A social worker may be praised by an employer for 'doing things right' but should always ask of themselves, 'Am I doing the right thing?'. This essential direction towards critical practice will help prevent taking (or not taking) action without thinking, which leads to knowledge of what we do but ignorance of why we do it.

Gough and McFadden (2001) would argue that a good starting point in adopting a critical approach is to acknowledge the social embeddedness of people's experience and behaviour and to recognize the way in which political, social and economic institutions can create, maintain and exacerbate inequality and oppression. A number of different theoretical ideas fall under the umbrella of the critical approach. These are drawn from Marxism, feminism, structuralism, anti-oppression and anti-racism. What they have in common is the proposition that social relations throughout social life are fashioned and regulated by macro-social structures such as capitalism, patriarchy and imperialism (Healy 2005). However, Brown and Rutter (2008) contend that the critical thinker will always tend to reject the concept of universal truth and question their own beliefs and views together with those of others and will challenge existing structures and dominant discourses in society while being open to new ideas. Social constructionism enables the critical thinker to understand how dominant discourse and so-called 'social facts' come into existence and thereby expose the contestable basis of their validity. For the individual student and practitioner the process of critical thinking can be a difficult and sometimes threatening task but nonetheless essential to anyone who seeks to be confident in their own minds that what they do is truly in the interests of those they are providing a service to. The critical social worker will seek to employ open-minded reflection secured in a commitment to social justice through anti-oppression and empowerment (Brechin et al. 2000).

A social work student recently made the following observation on social work practice in a written reflection on their practice placement experience: 'One can be forgiven for holding a view that the profession continues to delude itself by thinking that it is all empowering and caring because it claims to frame practice in terms of social justice or anti-racist constructs *when* it is aligned with authoritarian rather than libertarian policies in its role in implementing immigration policy' (anonymous). This is a very clear example of a situation where the demands of the professional role might be seen to conflict with the values held by a worker grounded in their political and ideological thinking. In order to make this critical reflective comment this student had to have a clear sense of their own views on the world they live in and their location in it, personally and professionally. The student has also demonstrated an understanding of social and political processes and their relationship to social work in a specific area of work together with a keen awareness of the situation of the service users in relation to the structures and institutions of society. Such seemingly straightforward statements can only be made from a position of deep insight and understanding. This book aims to help students and practitioners develop a framework for practice through the acquisition of the skills of insight and understanding through an exploration of the core thematic contexts of social work.

Key points

1   Social work students and practitioners need to be able to reflect on the professional role from a position of understanding at several levels.

2   Focusing on the application of knowledge through skills in social work practice can divert the student and practitioner from acquiring a deeper understanding of the practice environment.

3   A consideration of ideology, philosophy, values, power, social science and who constitute the service users is essential to developing effective critical practice.

4   Political, social and economic changes have transformed the discourse on society which threatens to negate awareness of the political and ideological context of professional activity in the public sector.

5   A critical approach to practice incorporates several theoretical ideas including Marxism, feminism, structuralism, post-modernism, anti-oppression and anti-racism.

Question for discussion

In what ways could social work be considered to be a political activity?

2 Establishing a world view

Why a 'world view'?

We exist in a social world and the experiences we have are a product of our interactions with many different individuals and organizations and the processes which define the relationships between these. Social work is involved in the lives of people for whom these interactions and processes have resulted in some form of difficulty, rendering day-to-day living seriously problematic. Those affected are rendered unable to use the resources available to them to resolve their problems without reference to supportive and caring services and, in some cases, punitive and corrective responses from societal institutions such as the courts.

David Howe (2009: 2), in his book *A Brief Introduction to Social Work Theory*, refers to the ways of making sense through which social workers can be helped to see 'regularities and familiar patterns in the muddle of practice'. He argues that developing a knowledge and understanding of theories of practice is essential to this process. In a similar way gaining a knowledge and understanding of the processes and patterns of the muddle of society can be seen as a necessary, first stage pre-requisite for being able to form a clear view of how people's problems arise both individually and collectively, and thereafter how they might be resolved. In other words the way in which we construct people's problems and the solutions we offer through our professional interventions will largely depend on our view of how the world we live in operates. We do not need to seek scientific proof of how society is organized but we should at least develop a clear idea of how we think society operates to gain a fuller understanding of the aetiology of the problems faced by service users and their lived experiences.

This raises the whole issue of the political nature of social work. If social work is concerned with people in their environments and people's environments are largely influenced by the decisions and policies of powerful social, governmental and economic institutions then social work is unavoidably tied into the political process. Social work is further embedded in politics by its relationship to the state (government) which, for the most part is the employer of social workers either directly or indirectly, and is the funder and manager of services and the overall strategist of social services through social policy and legislation. In working directly with people in difficulty who are most often the most deprived and marginalized in society while having direct and indirect connections with the state, social work is uniquely positioned to operate at different levels in the interests of service users. It is nonetheless the case that a number of social work students commence their studies claiming no knowledge of politics or, more worryingly, no interest in politics. The danger of such an approach is that one focuses on 'helping people' to the exclusion of consideration of the broader contexts within which this vocational task is carried out.

The motivation to help should not, in itself, be questioned as defective in some way, but the inclination to be satisfied with the personal interactions with service users in a micro-world of activity is severely limiting and potentially problematic for the professional social worker. Failing to acknowledge and comprehend wider contexts might serve to restrict the parameters of assessment therefore not providing the 'full picture' of a service user's situation. It will certainly influence the way problems are perceived particularly in the direction of 'individualizing' difficulties and 'victim blaming'. In the longer term this might, almost by default, help to reproduce the conditions which create and perpetuate the problems these very service users face from day to day. It is not just in the immediate world of experience that service users are confronted by exclusion, marginalization and oppression. It is also the case that in the wider societal contexts the forces of inequality, oppression and discrimination also operate to marginalize and exclude service users and influence professional practice.

While the direct activity in which social workers are engaged may protect the profession from accusations of being passive, it remains of significant importance that the profession avoid being attacked as philistine, as being 'content to live in a wholly unexplored world' (Davies 1968). The potential for such an accusation to be legitimately made against the social work profession is increased in proportion to the extent to which social work persists in concentrating its energy and attention on the detail of individual and interpersonal dynamics to the exclusion of thinking and actions directed at organizational and societal institutional structures. A combination of the two, recognizing the contribution of both personal action (agency) and structure, is more likely to result in a practice which properly addresses the two in proportionate measure. The possession of a world view based on an informed critical analysis of how society is ordered enables the social worker to think and act at several levels in a manner that better reflects the situational reality which service users, social workers and people generally find themselves in. Social workers need to be able to critically analyse themselves and their practice and be prepared to be openly accountable through being critically analysed by others. This can only be achieved through being able to explain why we do what we do in the various contexts within which we operate and within which service users experience their lives.

Process and structure

For the purpose of identifying or developing a world view it is necessary for us to switch our attention to macro-level structural arrangements within society. One route to understanding this is to consider living arrangements that the vast majority of people are familiar with. Most of us have experience of being brought up in a group living situation, often in one form or other of family or equivalent. We have or hear stories of how the experience of living with others as we develop leads to various personal experiences both positive and negative. The sharing of such narratives is an everyday occurrence in the arena of social work training. The interactions that take place in these groups determine and reflect the way in which the group becomes organized with individuals forming alliances, rules being made and power relationships and hierarchical arrangements being negotiated and created.

These arrangements or patterns of interacting can produce different outcomes and for some this can mean feeling excluded, undermined or abused by others within the situation. Umbarger (1983), in exploring the use of the systems paradigm in the micro level study of families, invites the reader to consider the relationship between structure and process. In this sense process refers to the sequence of individual behaviours and interactions/exchanges which take place between individuals in the family situation. If similar interactions take place and are repeated over time then the observer is able to identify 'patterns' indicating how the family sorts itself in terms of its personnel and what rules are set for the interactions that take place and the tasks it performs. These form the 'structures' of the family. When we later consider the formation of social structures the family will be located as a prominent institutional structure itself (albeit in diverse forms) in many societies globally.

In thinking of society as similarly comprising process and structure we can begin to see that viewing it this way allows us to develop a picture and gives us a greater chance of making sense of how society is ordered and operates. It is a much bigger project than looking at small group living situations, of course, and immensely complex as evidenced by the considerable literature and longstanding theoretical debates that stand testimony to the task involved. Knuttila and Kubik (2000) state that human beings have individual and collective needs, drives and problems and that they act purposefully and socially to address these. Social arrangements and structures necessarily become a significant part of human existence and experience as these same structures become strong determinants of human interaction and behaviour. How we interact determines the nature and type of social structures created and these, in turn, determine the way we interact with and behave towards each other. This relationship between agency and structure is central to an understanding of the situation and actions of service users and the social work response to these.

The challenge here, as professionals and critical thinkers, is to make a significant adjustment to our position and to see from outside as well as from within. Social workers need to be highly skilled at both working within and seeing from without. Howe (2009) illustrates this effectively through the analogy of balloonists in the eighteenth century. Soaring above the seemingly random, chaotic world they had launched from they now saw order and the world took shape before their eyes. The structure of their world became evident.

Now Howe was not suggesting that all social workers should take courses in ballooning or that it should be included in the social work curriculum but they most certainly should be encouraged by the fact that in all the chaos and turmoil (process) of everyday practice there are patterns in social activity and arrangements (structure) which can provide significant insight into the aetiology, maintenance and resolution of the social problems that conspire to undermine the life chances of so many. This is not an either/or situation; it is a chaos within order situation. The two are linked in a process of exchange and the aim is to understand how each has an impact on the other. The challenge is to develop strategies to secure one's position in the turmoil while freeing oneself to explore the order of things. In accepting this challenge we need to recognize that we are 'usually dominated by the mental shortcuts [we] use to make sense of the world ... individuals tend to look for ways to process information quickly and rely on cues within new information to tell them how to connect it with the images of the world they already have' (Gilligan 2007: 736). In acknowledging this we can begin to free ourselves up to think about and see things in different ways.

Cohesion and conflict

In analysing human interaction and structural arrangements in society we can begin to develop insight into the nature of the relationships between individuals, groups, communities, institutions and the state. Part of the process of socialization for each of us is to develop a sense of belonging to a society or nation implying that we are all part of an essentially homogeneous machine operating for the good of all its members. Our family, religious, legal, education and work systems, in most instances, deliver this message as we journey through our developmental years. At whatever stage we find ourselves, the importance of cohesion and organization through common goals is presented as the reality that we should adhere to and divert from at our peril. There might be any number of realities which present some very different images of how the world we are part of operates but the opportunity to acquire knowledge of these alternatives may be limited. Stability is considered an essential ingredient in sustaining the existence of any group or system and the suggestion that there are other fundamental ways of doing things can threaten stability in any situation.

I can hear the voices of colleagues over the years complaining either of how change is such a slow process in any of the organizations they have worked in or how disruptive yet superficial change is when it is introduced. Paradoxically change does take place and has been the mantra of management from the late twentieth century and is increasingly so with the emergence of the business model and market oriented approaches in public sector organizations. Continuous reorganization, increased bureaucracy, managerialism, de-professionalization of the workforce, down-sizing, target setting, performance criteria and service user involvement have all been introduced in the name of modernization and improved service quality. The divide in wealth and income in society has nonetheless increased over this period and the relative social and economic position of the greater majority of service users has worsened. In such circumstances change serves to re-enforce the given system rather than challenge it. The 'shuffling the deckchairs on the Titanic' syndrome has rendered the kinds of change we have witnessed of little use in moving towards a more socially just, egalitarian and empowering society. We can see a parallel here with one of Eileen Munro's (2011a) conclusions in her interim report on the review of child protection in England. She makes the observation that the question which is always asked is whether people have followed procedures, not whether procedures have brought any benefit to children.

The continuing drive towards common purpose and consensus in society can often cloud the debate as to whether cohesion or conflict characterize the society we live in. The question this poses goes to the root of attempts to explain the processes which lead to people finding themselves in poverty, marginalized, victimized, exploited, deprived or abused. Are these people the accidents of a society moving together in one direction but making mistakes, or are they necessary side products of a society characterized by competing interests and conflicting aims? Whether we see society as ordered or in conflict is important as they represent two entirely different ways of thinking about what is happening. The framework we use to perceive what is going on depends to a large degree on which of these we adopt.

Those who fall on the cohesion or order side of the debate have long argued for a *functionalist* view of society where the function of the activities of human beings, organizations and institutions is to achieve integration and stability around agreed aims, goals and values. Within this position, nonetheless, is recognition of the potential for internal stresses within society to threaten this stability. In the seventeenth century Thomas Hobbes (2008) made claim to humans being essentially self seeking and the avoidance of a 'war of all against all' as only possible through humanity subscribing to a higher authority in the form of legitimate centralized government which would provide order and stability as individuals pursued their own ends. As the champion of order the government has to be respected and largely unchallenged. Strong government becomes highly desirable and the more the governed give their consent the stronger the government. Interestingly the question of strength (power) being in some way dependent on the coercive capabilities of government is omitted here as it is assumed that legitimacy through consent precludes the need for such armoury. For other theorists government does not so much stand outside of society as an independent arbitration system but is an integral part of the process of harmonization. Emile Durkheim (Knuttila and Kubik 2000) proposes that individual 'wants' arise from the social order. He suggested that an 'organic solidarity' is formed in modern industrial societies through the interdependence of individuals and institutions, which is characteristic of the division of labour into many diverse and specialist activities in the process of economic production. Each *function* is in some way dependent on the others and so we become morally obliged to serve the whole *structure*. Individual 'wants' become collective or shared goals which are legitimate and desirable. The state serves to provide strong moral authority to control any tendency to individual or institutional conflict thrown up by increasing diversity of activity in advanced industrial society. People fulfil their economic and social roles in the way they do, not only because they are prescribed for them but because they come to believe that this is the right way for social and economic relationships to be arranged.

This human action was a central concern for Talcott Parsons in his theorizing on society as a system and its need to resolve the problems it faces in order to survive. Human action, for Parsons (1969), has a natural tendency to lead to conflict and disorganization in a significant grouping such as society. Through his development of the theory of structural functionalism it is possible to identify some key common features of the functionalist approach to understanding society. These include 'the establishment and articulation of collective goals, and various forms of social regulation are viewed as the basis of system survival' (Knuttila and Kubik 2000: 47). The regulation of society is achieved through the institutions of that society working in harmony with the requirements of the social system for the maintenance of the whole. These institutions or sub-systems include the economy, government, family, education, religion and culture, which together work to ensure integration.

In these circumstances the consequences for individuals failing to act in a way that promotes integration can be severe. Mullaly (1997) points to one of the inevitable consequences of seeing the institutions of society as necessarily good and correct and their controlling function to be a requirement for stability. Such a stance leads 'order theorists to conclude that social problems are best described and understood by focusing on lower levels or plateaus of society than on the societal or structural level' (p. 121). As Howe (1987) suggests, if people do not perform and behave in a way that promotes the common aims, goals and duties they are seen as 'poor functioners' (p. 36) and, 'Police, social workers, and officials of all kinds become interested in those who stray from the established standards of good conduct, self-care and financial independence' (p. 36). If the interventions of these bodies are unsuccessful then the individuals concerned are further treated as deviants, excluded from mainstream society and seen as a threat to the established order of things. Exclusion not only removes the threat but also acts as an example to others and thereby a deterrent to deviation from established norms of behaviour.

If social cohesion is achieved through the presentation of 'the way things are' in society as being correct and necessary then any problems that people experience will not be seen as a fault in the system but as a fault or failing in the people concerned. Individuals will be seen as the source of their own poverty or emotional problems. Families will be seen as the source of many forms of dysfunctional behaviour and particular groups such as disaffected youth as the source of their own dissatisfaction and exclusion. A failure to 'fit in' becomes the primary diagnosis and the resolution therefore lies in helping those affected to 'fit in' once again through being fixed or corrected in some way. From a functionalist perspective social work has to operate as an integrating force within existing social arrangements so will itself be largely engineered to provide the means for people to re-integrate or 'fit in' to the existing order. It is clear that many of social work's methods are in fact designed to intervene at individual, familial and sub-cultural levels and not directed at wider organizational and structural elements of society. Payne (2005) offers evidence for this in claiming that statutory social work interventions are largely of an 'individualist-reformist' type whereby individuals are assisted to adapt to the world they live in. Major social work methods such as task-centred approaches, cognitive behavioural therapy and person-centred approaches all derive from this particular view of social problems.

A different perspective is offered by those who see conflict as the feature which best characterizes society as opposed to cohesion and order. This approach incorporates the views of those who subscribe to Marxist, socialist, radical and critical ways of analysing society. On joining social work in the mid-1970s I was met with a stern warning that a senior manager had identified a small group of card carrying Marxist social work recruits whose activities would be closely monitored! This exemplifies the way in which non-mainstream views can stir up apprehension and threat and the terms used to represent these views be used pejoratively. For the conflict theorist society, while being made up of interacting parts, is not bound by a consensus of values, aims and actions. It is made up of groups competing for power and resources with different interests, values and goals which bring them into opposition to each other.

If we consider economic power in society a major analysis is offered by Karl Marx who proposed that class structures built around ownership results in some groups becoming dominant and powerful and having interests which are in direct conflict with those groups lacking in ownership and power (Joseph 2006). For the functionalist these inequalities of power and ownership are considered a natural and normal social arrangement which need only be tempered at the extremes. In Marxist thinking they go to the core of inequality and poverty in both material and psychological terms. For Marxists class is determined by social relations arising from economic arrangements in capitalism. Those who own the means of producing goods or delivering services use this position for the purpose of making profit from the sale of goods and provision of services which are produced and staffed by workers and machinery which the owners hire and own respectively. In order to maximize profit the cost of hiring workers (labour) and other production costs have to be kept as low as possible so that the price of goods and services both exceeds the cost of production and is affordable to customers. The primary goal of capitalist production of the pursuit of profit leads to the employee or worker being exploited as the wage they receive is less than the value of the fruits of their labour. The interests of capitalism are therefore served by maintaining a low wage and low tax economy in which unemployment offers a downward pressure on wages and salaries as those in work make fewer claims for improvements in conditions for fear of losing their jobs when so many are trying to obtain work.

Although there are many income levels within modern capitalist societies and the class system may appear more complicated than envisaged in Marx's theory, it remains the case that many millions of people in western economies find themselves in either low paid, poorly protected employment or unemployed and this results in persistent and high levels of relative poverty. This situation is exacerbated by the addition of discrimination, prejudice and oppression whereby certain groups including those belonging to black and ethnic minorities, people with disabilities and older people find themselves more likely to be relatively impoverished through poorer pay and working conditions or unemployment. As Howe (1987: 142) suggests, from a conflict perspective the capitalist economy 'produces profoundly unequal economic relationships between the ruling class and the working class'. It might be that in modern society many find it difficult to locate themselves in terms of the ruling class/working class divide but this should not detract from addressing and acknowledging the reality of profound economic inequality that exists and persists and blights the lives of so many.

Capitalism sustains itself by ensuring the maintenance of sufficient consumers to purchase its products and services (demand), and as it spreads across the globe and the easier movement of capital and labour to lower cost locations is facilitated then it is more able to sustain itself. It is nonetheless the case that the tension between lowering costs and maintaining demand presents major problems, when people who are relatively impoverished by the process grow in number and purchase fewer products and/or production grows to a level which outstrips demand so stocks grow and sales fall. The outcome of this process is falling profits, slowed production, failing businesses, mass redundancies and rising unemployment. What we experience are cyclical rises and falls in the wealth of societies and the consequent uncertainty and increased problems for people in times of recession. Not everyone is affected to the same degree and it is the case that people make choices in their lives and that education and application can contribute in a small way to upward mobility within a society. Nonetheless, looking at the economic process systemically it is possible to conclude that certain inequalities and deprivation are themselves products of the system and that 'human agency is exercised within social relationships that take on the character of overarching structures' (Holton 1997: 27). From a conflict perspective it is argued that social work within advanced capitalism will continue to work with people whose circumstances are primarily created by the system they live in even if some of the choices they make might worsen those circumstances.

Conflicting interests and competing groups in society are a matter of economic class for the Marxist but such an approach does not satisfactorily explain the diversity of social divisions present in today's society. We are introduced to the complementary (or perhaps rival) concept to class of 'status' in the writings of Max Weber. While economic class can be seen as deriving from the mechanisms of the market, status stratification offers a much wider instance of 'the unremitting struggle for power amongst rival groups' (Callinicos 1999: 164). Although the domination of some over others remains an important factor, a more complex picture of power relationships emerges. The tendency towards closed groupings along lines of, among others, religion, ethnicity, gender and geographical location supports a continuing struggle for power and results in the exclusion and oppression of certain groups. It could also be argued that this same tendency discourages different groups from recognizing and acknowledging commonalities around social experience such as poverty and therefore diverts attention away from these when it comes to governmental responses and the development of policies to address social problems.

The excluded or marginalized in society are viewed in significantly different ways depending on the perspective adopted. For the functionalist the damaging effect on society of people falling outside of the commonly held cohesive values, goals and activities which bind us through consensus can result in 'anomie', a condition where cohesion is splintered, uncertainty reigns, social disorganization ensues and system survival is threatened. For the conflict theorist the structure of economy and social institutions 'alienate' people by separating them from the products of their work and from each other and commodifies them as labour for hire. The system survives by alienating and dividing people with the owners of wealth and powerful in society employing the institutions of society to set the parameters for acceptable thought and behaviour. The functionalist sees people as the creators of anomie and the conflict theorist sees the system as the creator of alienation. The solution to anomie is to bring individuals back into the consensus based social fold; the solution to alienation is to change society to remove inequality, exclusion and alienation (Mullaly 1997).

Attempts to develop a world view are further complicated by the influence of post-modern thinking with its emphasis on subjective experience as offering a better understanding of reality. This has led to the conclusion that there are endless ways of interpreting and understanding the world and each is of equal value. The theoretical task of objectively trying to understand society undertaken by functionalists and conflict theorists is rejected and effectively rendered redundant as social reality outside of subjective experience does not exist. Myers (2010) challenges this by questioning the ability of the new found cultural identity and celebration of diversity to 'create the material basis for wellbeing and freedom when business owners choose to hoard their capital instead of creating jobs' (p. 133). Social work should not be faced with the choice of accepting one or other of a grand single structural determinant of social division as opposed to a diverse labyrinth of group or individual based divisions. It should be charged with working at several levels and designing interventions that resolve the inequalities experienced in common across disadvantaged groups in society. Imaginative and productive practice is more likely to arise from a position which promotes the complementarity of competing theoretical concepts within a clear framework of thinking and ideas grounded in an awareness of conflicting interests and power relations.

Awareness and hegemony

To begin to establish a practice strategy that can effectively create the opportunity for social change then it is important to not only understand the patterns of social, political and economic relations in society (structure) but also to have some insight into how they are maintained and change resisted. Antonio Gramsci, a Marxist philosopher, developed the concept of hegemony which directs our attention to the need for those in leadership and authority positions in society to maintain control not by coercion alone but by being able to gain the consent of the members of society. Jonathan Joseph (2006: 52) describes the process involved: 'Hegemony corresponds to the construction, organisation and distribution of this consensus through and beyond the state and civil society.'

For Gramsci (1971) it is not sufficient simply to gain power in government in an advanced democratic country with a strong civil society comprising institutions including the education, law and order, religious, media and familial systems. It is necessary for these to possess similar and common goals for a social and political consensus to be achieved. Social work is, of course, part of institutional civil society and is therefore subject to the same mechanism. A relatively short leap of critical thinking can lead to seeing how this might account, at least in part, for the emphasis in social work in advanced western society to focus on individual and familial change to solve social problems at the personal level.

It is through being in positions of influence and power within the institutions of civil society that one is able to engineer the process of hegemony and achieve consensus around a particular set of beliefs and goals (ideology). Through this process people in society subscribe to the rules of the established order as a result of submission, an element of which is the tendency of many to detach themselves from the business of politics and social governance. A lack of interest in the wider political and social processes should not be seen wholly as an autonomous, deliberate act of the independent minded individual but rather as part of a process which assists those in power to maintain the status quo. This is not to say that the general public and social workers are mindless automatons but it is dangerous not to appreciate that we are influenced by more subtle social processes which, by definition, do not necessarily nor readily reveal themselves to us. People can come to know and accept their place in society without seriously questioning this.

Once established, the prevailing way of thinking about people and society (ideology) becomes institutionalized itself and therefore highly resistant to change. This is not to say that there are not differences and disputes between and within different groupings and institutions in society but it is to argue that the prevailing overall economic, social and political arrangements are supported and largely unchallenged. The role of the government (state) in this arena has been a matter for great debate. As we have seen from a functionalist (consensus) perspective, the state is seen as being given legitimacy through consensus, serving as a neutral body with the task of maintaining order and cohesion in the face of residual deviance or other threats to stability. For conflict theorists the state is given an integral position in a society of oppositional interests. While it retains relative autonomy through its several functions (Miliband 1977) including economic, consensus maintaining (ideological-cultural), law and order and protecting the national interest (international policy), it is also central in facilitating and reinforcing the existing economic relationships within capitalist society. The extent to which it mediates and directs the resolution of disputes and differences within society is determined by its actions being consistent with this overall aim (Poulantzas 1976). In this sense it can be seen as part of the hegemonic process without being identified simply as the mouthpiece of any ruling class or elite.

If we take the example of wealth distribution in society we can see how the state's role takes effect within capitalist society. Governments in a number of western capitalist countries, since the mid-twentieth century on, have declared wars of one type or another on poverty. At the same time the mechanism of capitalist production relentlessly concentrates the ownership of the vast majority of a country's wealth in a few hands and governments see the global market 'as the final, and unchallengeable arbiter in economic – and ultimately in social – life' and welcome it as 'the main provider' (Jones and Novak 1999: 181). The great majority of the populations is kept on the periphery and disallowed from meaningful participation. The clear conflict of interest between those with and those without is mediated by government through policies which provide limited financial benefit to the poor together with educational and training encouragement and sanctions geared towards them obtaining employment. The issue of the major redistribution of a nation's resources is circumvented and the focus switched to the inefficacy, inadequacy and indolence of the poor themselves, thus preserving the sense of the system as able to provide so long as people are willing to and know how to partake properly by making the most of the opportunities presented to them. These are the people, the poor in society, who constitute the significant majority of social work's service users irrespective of which particular client group they belong to. The dominant, wealth-owning group in society retains its position as the main beneficy of the system while the remainder of the population accept the prevailing unequal social order.

Georg Lukacs (1971) reminds us that we lose awareness of the way in which society is constructed through social relationships and that we come to see society and its content as somehow independent and separate from us. He refers to this as 'reification'. We respond to society as a fixed entity and fail to see the processes that construct it. In not seeing society as a whole we are unable to understand it other than in terms of our own fragment of experience. For Lukacs, 'The reification of society and therefore consciousness means that we often do not see things as interconnected and we struggle to see the totality of things' (Joseph 2006: 59). The challenge for social workers is to 'become aware of ourselves as socio-historical beings who must act in order to change things' (p. 58).

The way in which language reinforces a particular way of seeing things (discourse) is also worthy of consideration. Jurgen Habermas has written extensively on the role of discourse in the maintenance of power differentials in society. Inequalities and control are sustained by the manipulation of communication by powerful interests (Outhwaite 2009). It is possible to discern the dominant modes of thinking on issues through analysing the words used and the discursive agendas set by governments, the media and other powerful groups in society on certain social issues. For example when there is an economic crisis and unemployment rises significantly it is invariably the case that the agenda moves to focusing on the unemployed themselves and categories of 'the work shy', 'scroungers' and 'lacking work skills' dominate with the associated solutions of greater surveillance, reform of the welfare state towards restricted eligibility, cutting benefits, re-assessments and reducing access to services being the preferred options. The alternative discourse focusing on tax avoidance and evasion, city bonuses, bank profits and fiscal and monetary inequality is given much less prominence and features much less in tangible government policy. Habermas looks forward to the realization of 'communicative competence' through which people will be free to enter into informed discourse without these forms of distortion of communication. In these circumstances people within civil society will arrive at consensus and truth and overcome vested interest in a truly participatory democracy. The technology to support this type and scale of communication with the potential to directly challenge the ideology of the powerful is increasingly present globally. The quality of the communication as measured against Habermas's 'communicative competence' is yet to be determined but there is a place for the professional social work to enter the discourse from a position of self-awareness, informed knowledge and political sophistication.

Paradigms: frameworks for thought and practice

In building our 'world view' it will undoubtedly prove helpful to have frameworks of thinking to which we can refer, to help clarify our understanding of what it is we see and experience going on in the world. Howe (1992: 22) defines the concept of a paradigm as used in the social sciences as constituting 'all the assumptions, theories, beliefs, values and methods that make up a particular and preferred view of the world'. This follows on from the work of Thomas Kuhn who proposed the concept of 'paradigms' in his book, *The Structure of Scientific Revolutions* ([1962] 1996) in which they are presented as models or frameworks derived from the prevailing or dominant state of knowledge and theory in science at any point in history and how this influences the way problems and their solutions are researched and understood until new paradigms arise. Knowledge of different paradigms and a recognition of that which is dominant not only offer the social worker a coherent way of viewing the world but also afford the social work profession the opportunity to locate itself in the world within which it operates, to clarify its beliefs and values and work for change consistent with these.

Howe goes on to offer an analysis of social work theory and methods deploying the work of Burrell and Morgan (1979) in which they construct a four paradigm grid for analysing social theory. They suggest two significant dimensions for viewing society, these being objective/subjective and regulation/radical change. With the former dimension one chooses to see reality as either something which can be observed (objective) or arising purely from the experience of the individual (subjective). By way of example, for the one poverty can be seen and defined by external material measurement; for the other it can only be present if it exists in the mind of the individual. In the case of the latter dimension one sees society as either ordered through the consensus of its members around shared values, aims, goals and interests or as inherently divided through a state of conflict of interests and inequality of resources, power and influence.

When combined the dimensions create four paradigms; Radical Humanists (subjective radical change approach), Radical Structuralists (objective radical change approach), Interpretavists (subjective regulation approach), and Functionalists (objective regulation approach). The first two relate to a conflict view of society and the second two to a cohesive view. The suggestion is that the paradigms are incompatible and that certain ways of working are derived from each paradigm and mutually inconsistent. Howe (1992) adapts these to categorize different social work methods by linking them to one or other of the four approaches defined. This may prove helpful in reflecting on how the methods we use are directly related to the way we see the world operating for our service users but the language used results in the 'conflict' based approaches being deemed alternative or 'other' and defined in relation to the dominant consensus paradigms (Deetz 1996). This makes them less accessible and difficult to take into ownership by mainstream professions such as social work and precludes the use of compatible parallel interventions which alleviate individual anxiety and suffering while challenging societal processes and structures. It is the case that within any discipline more than one paradigm might co-exist but it is evident that the 'regulation' based paradigms dominate in social work practice in western industrial societies. It is only when the anomalies confronting the dominant paradigm, such as continuing and worsening inequality and oppression, become either so great in quantity or unable to be explained in terms of the existing order that the dominant paradigm changes or is discarded for a new one (Kuhn [1962] 1996).

In his analysis of social work approaches Payne (2005) identifies three paradigmatic views presented as the three points of a triangle: the 'reflexive-therapeutic', the 'socialist-collectivist' and the 'individualist-reformist'. This offers a fluid space which allows for the simultaneous location of practice in changeable proximity to each of the paradigmatic views and for the direction of intervention to range from the individual through to the structural. The social worker is able to move between them using the associated methods according to their fit to best achieving the desired outcomes. Payne argues that the three 'views' or 'minor paradigms' in relationship defines the current paradigm of social work because it accounts for all social work theory and practice and the debates which take place on their respective merits. For Payne social work is a social construction derived from the debate and exchanges of views on what constitutes it. The only agreed view in social work which defines a paradigm is the acceptance of different opinions on the way social work should be. This might reflect the debates within social work but there is still the problem of addressing the location of social work itself in the wider scheme of things, which directly influences the relative strength of each 'view' both in terms of the outcome of the debate and its translation into practice methods which are most prominent at any one point in time.

When presenting paradigmatic structures to social work students the question often asked is whether it is not possible to mix and match the approaches as social work is considered to be eclectic. Perhaps one of the reasons that social work has done little historically to reduce the social problems and inequality with which it deals on a day-to-day basis is its perceived neutrality in promoting the eclectic approach. Poulter (2005), in promoting heuristic practice, warns that a non-reflective eclecticism leads to social workers applying a mix of theories within a functionalist framework resulting in their acting as agents of social control. He argues for the addition of a Heuristic Paradigm which would incorporate theoretical approaches derived from professional's reflection on their interaction with individuals in each unique situation. While such an analysis does offer hope for a practice more oriented to 'agency' within 'structure' it is difficult to see how the structural dimension is accommodated through the methods cited such as constructive social work, collaborative advocacy, recovery work and symbolic interactionist approaches. These methods are largely individual or do not extend beyond small scale community work.

By turning to the use of paradigms to identify the social and political context of social work we should be able to articulate different forms of ideology, different ways of constructing social problems, different views on how the welfare state should operate and the different methods of social work intervention associated with each paradigm. Since the emergence of the New Right in western politics in the 1980s the paradigm which has directed our political and economic life is that of neo-liberalism. This is interchangeably referred to as neo-conservatism. Jones and Novak (1999) title this period the 'neo-liberal project'. The underlying aim is to shift the balance of economic, social and political power firmly towards capital and its institutional sympathizers. The market becomes the arbiter of economic and social life and the role of the state is minimized. The welfare state and the growing acceptance of diversity in race, sexuality and family life are presented as major threats to our way of life and economy and a return to traditional values, strong families, individual responsibility and hard work supported by a market-based meritocracy are the key to rescuing us from a serious crisis. Turning to the inherent fragilities of the capitalist system as the source of crisis is not an option in this way of thinking. The universal appeal of such a position is at least in part due to the failure of the state to offer solutions to those in need in increasingly bureaucratized, under resourced and restrictive systems of service provision. The ferocity of attacks on welfare provision and state services therefore resonates not only with those who have little call on the state but also those who are heavily dependent on it for survival. The irony lies in the fact that this same project has overseen large increases in wealth disparities between rich and poor within nations and globally and the freeing up of the market through de-regulation and other measures has resulted in the biggest financial crisis (the global banking crisis of 2008 on) to face the global economy in recent history. An interesting twist to the neo-liberal project is the resulting public ownership of several financial institutions required to stave off a complete collapse of the financial system. This has, however, not resulted in any significant structural change to financial operations.

The neo-liberal (neo-conservative) paradigm espouses the free-market, inequality, individualism, minimal residual state involvement and the surveillance and social control of the poor and other deviants (Mullaly 1997). Without inequality there is no motivation for individuals to better themselves. People are held responsible for their own failure (or success) and social work is largely directed towards correcting failing individuals and families and investigations to prevent abuse. Mullaly goes on to contrast several paradigms including Liberalism, Social Democracy and Marxism. The latter two place far more emphasis on the belief in collectivism and collaboration over individualism, the importance of government intervention and public ownership of economic resources, the more equal distribution of wealth and resources and the root of social problems lying in the inherently conflictual capitalist system. The role of social work here is re-focused on supporting service users as casualties of the system and acting with them and others collaboratively to restructure society.

The liberalism paradigm is presented as a humanitarian softer version of neo-liberalism with a mixed economy approach. This equates to the 'Third Way' introduced in Britain by the 'New Labour' government in the late 1990s following on from Bill Clinton's pronouncements in the USA (Jones and Novak 1999). The destructive elements of capitalism were to be tempered with greater state intervention while retaining the essential competitiveness and market oriented approach of capitalist production and distribution. Community and the cohesive civic society (communitarianism) would replace the individualism of the 'new right' with an individualism characterized by positive social and community involvement and responsibility. Government provides the opportunities and individuals carry the responsibility to take those opportunities. The existing economic system is still seen as the best provider of prosperity and increasing living standards. The 'Third Way' places social work in the position of helping bring people back in from the margins of society in a process of social inclusion by correction, guidance and support. Individuals remain responsible for grasping opportunities or not and the state takes responsibility for creating the infra-structure of opportunity.

Where do you stand?

Ferguson and Lavalette (2004) make the observation that post-modern thinking and its promotion of diversity of truth and subjectivity is not particularly helpful in moving social work forward in pursuing social justice and emancipatory practice as it tends to disallow taking a position on issues of political, social and economic significance while retaining an emphasis on cultural identity and individualism, so resonant with right wing conservative politics and policies. Mullaly (1997), while pointing to the useful critiques of modernism within the post-modern perspective, remarks that post-modernism fails to recognize the continuing realities of the modern world in the form of global capitalism and political ideology. It can be argued that the inclusion of post-modern ideas in social work theory and methods renders more difficult the ability of the professional to take a clear position on the inequality and oppression which confronts them each day in their practice as these concepts become fragmented and localized. It might be true to contend that 'the assertion of cultural identity has been powerless in the face of growing economic inequality, both within sovereign states and between them. Ethnic or racial pride cannot create the material basis for well being and freedom when business owners choose to hoard their capital instead of creating jobs' (Myers 2010: 133). Nonetheless a more positive interpretation can be constructed by drawing elements of the modern and the post-modern together. Giddens (1997) acknowledges that post-modernism has not replaced modernism and many of the institutions of modernism remain in what he refers to as 'high modernity' with both its positive and its negative aspects.

As the two co-exist it is important to consider the impact of both and their potential contribution to achieving the aims of a critical social work practice. A knowledge and analysis of diversity has brought with it new levels of awareness for many members of oppressed groups in society, albeit along different dimensions to the 'grand narratives' of structural theories. This would suggest that the more detailed the appreciation of the part that the 'agency' of individual actors plays in social processes is, the more likely it is able to realize the potential for change through recognition of commonalities in the face of powerful and resistant structural forces. This does not deny taking a position on inequality and oppression but posits adopting an approach which might challenge these through the effective use of 'agency' within 'structure'. Massive inequalities of power have not repelled people from struggling against the prevailing order and winning concessions from the state throughout history. Macro-level thinking provides the 'join' for the fragmentation of post-modern approaches which many celebrate and many lament. As I write the peoples of several states in the Middle East are rising up against regimes which they see as having maintained levels of inequality which are no longer tolerable. These situations are made complex by religious, tribal, ethnic and other divisions but it is possible to discern the unifying force as the dissatisfaction with the persistent concentration of wealth and power and enduring high levels of economic and social injustice which many millions have experienced.

If we step back and analyse the location of social work in wider social processes and structures we can develop a world view which can help equip the profession to avoid the consequence that Althusser warns of: 'Those groups lacking independence and autonomy will be ideologically subordinate to the hegemonic group and will adopt their world-view as their own' (in Joseph 2006: 55). Working at the heart of inequality and exclusion places social work at the centre of political life and bestows on the profession some obligation to be democratically active through challenging rather than acquiescing. The alternative is the kind of democracy in which 'the people choose leaders whom they trust. Then the chosen leaders say, "Now shut your mouths and obey. The people . . . are no longer free to interfere in the leaders' business"', (Weber

2009: 653). Our own everyday experiences reveal the secrecy and inaccessibility of modern-day government in a representative democracy. We are discouraged from too energetic participation in the affairs of state. Witness the use of instruments of coercion in this country to quell mass demonstrations from the so-called 'poll tax riots', through the anti-Iraq war marches and the student opposition to increased student fees. Add the frustration of observing the drawn out process of 'inquiries' into these matters, with their restricted terms of reference preventing the public dissemination of key information and we can ponder the nature of the democracy we live in. This has a direct bearing on the propensity for change within society when the goal of social and economic justice is sought in the interests of the poorest and most vulnerable.

Given that social work intervenes mostly in the lives of poor people then the establishment of an independent and autonomous view of how society operates has to include clear thinking on the creation and maintenance of poverty as a social division on a macro-level together with an understanding of the experience of marginalization at a personal level. The distribution of material resources has a direct impact on the individual's ability to exercise free choice in the various aspects of their lives and to realize their capabilities through being more able to collaborate with others (Myers 2010). If social work is to promote social egalitarianism then it has to turn its attention to the way the economy is organized and operates. This is not to deny the relevance and significance of other social divisions, people's experiences and the promotion and support of diversity, but to re-position poverty and inequality at the forefront of social work concerns. As Myers (2010: 133) states: 'A theory of history that takes seriously the material constraints and possibilities of our world is better equipped than its competitors to explain the origins of inequality and the most effective strategies for combating it.' Chris Jones (2002) has previously pointed to the manner in which the obvious relationship between poverty and social work has been largely ignored in the discourse on social work practice. As social work includes the aim of achieving social justice and social change in the definition of its task (IFSW 2000) then it is necessary that social workers acquire a clear set of beliefs and understanding of how the world operates consistent with this aim.

Key points

1 How we construct people's problems and the solutions we offer directly reflects our understanding of how the world we live in operates even if we are not aware of it.

2 Social work is a political activity by virtue of its relationship to the state and its relationship to service users.

3 Social structures have a strong influence on human interaction and behaviour.

4 The 'functionalist perspective' constructs personal and social problems as the failings and inadequacies of individuals and families. The 'conflict perspective' constructs personal and social problems as a product of social structures and processes.

5 Government can be seen as either the legitimate arbiter of social disputes and conflicts or as integral to supporting the current dominant economic and social arrangements in society.
6 Paradigms provide frameworks for thinking which help us to better understand the way society operates. They also assist in locating social work and its methods socially and politically.
7 It is possible to take elements of modernism and post-modernism to effect a social work practice which addresses inequality and injustice.

Questions for discussion

1 How is the construction of personal and social problems seen differently by the 'cohesive' and 'conflict' views of society?
2 What are the strengths and weaknesses of the 'modern' and 'post-modern' perspectives in attempts to understand society and social and individual problems?
3 Poor people constitute the significant majority of service users. In what ways does current social work practice address poverty as a social problem?

3 Values in social work

Introduction

Please, take a seat in the 'uneasy' chair. This is not the one you flop into at the end of a gruelling day and relax as the fabric folds around you. This is the one that makes you jolt forward and look back wondering whether it is your body or the chair that denies you that comfortable feeling. No matter how many positions you try or how often you sit back thinking you have achieved comfort, you can never quite settle. In social work, values operate very much as this uneasy chair does, repeatedly challenging you to make sense of what values are, how they are applied in practice and the many dilemmas which arise in trying to reconcile what confronts you and how you respond to it with what you believe to be good and right.

On a personal level striving for consistency between thought, words and actions is a major task in itself. In moments of honest reflection we may admit to struggling with this. In addition there is our understanding of what the role and purpose of professional social work in society is or should be and how this fits with our own aims and intentions in being social workers. This is further complicated by working in organizations with their own missions, aims and objectives which may or may not conflict with our own aims and aspirations. Then there is the more abstract question of social work knowledge and how this is constructed both at a theoretical and practical level.

Shardlow (2009) has grouped these areas for consideration into 'restricted', 'mid-range' and 'broad' dimensions demonstrating the range of subject matter covered in analysing values. These include philosophy, politics, ethics, theology and epistemology. So, not an easy task lies ahead if one is to at least satisfy oneself that they have explored the issue sufficiently. Shardlow also likens trying to grasp social work values and ethics to 'picking up a live, large and very wet fish out of a running stream' (p. 23), which you are destined never to hold on to even if you manage to initially lift one. Sara Banks (2006) similarly refers to 'values' as a vague term which appears to have a number of different meanings.

It sometimes isn't presented as such a difficult subject as many times I have read in student essays the stated adherence to anti-oppressive practice, person-centred approaches and honesty at all times to name a few. Many students feel an obligation to confirm their value base in this way as they feel it is expected of them and the scope of their essays may disallow a fuller examination of their declarations. So long as values are presented in 'list' forms to students and practitioners by professional and governmental bodies then there is a tendency to replicate these through communication in various quarters as commonsense approaches within caring professions.

It is often in practice that students find themselves immersed in the complexity of values for the first time. One described to me her worrying anticipation of becoming a qualified, registered practitioner and finding herself located in a different position in the professional hierarchy. Her distress arose from her experience of multi-professional/agency practice both in her placement and her paid work. She had found that all too often the workers – who had most direct knowledge of their service users, let alone the service users themselves – were excluded from discussion and decision making merely by virtue of their position in this hierarchy. This not only contradicted her beliefs about the worth of people but raised issues about the structure of organizations, societal and cultural mores, the fit between personal, professional and organizational values and the nature of social work knowledge and activity. The student was concerned that she might become absorbed into working in this way. She retained a determination not to do so, in large part based on a relatively clear and detailed idea of what she meant by her stated values and how these should translate into practice. She nonetheless realized that her perception and understanding could be clouded by circumstance and appreciated that the professionals and organizations she was critiquing would probably make equal claim to ethically sound practice.

Values and ethics

When talking about values in the context of human relationships and professional activity the intention is usually to define the preferred way to view human beings and our approaches and responses in entering working relationships with them. This is invariably based on our existing beliefs. In this sense values are defined differently to when we wish to place a value on an object, such as the value of one car relative to another car. However in expressing a preference arising from our valuations in either case we discover a common feature of values; that is, that they are an expression of preference whatever the reference point. I might prefer this car to that car and I might prefer to show people respect rather than disrespect them.

The idea of preference being at the core of values renders the nature of values subject to the vagaries of human choice at personal, communal and cultural levels. This then makes it difficult to lay claim to one set of values being 'right' when compared to others as there is no objective benchmark against which to measure the relative validity of different value sets. All values are human constructions whether personal, organizational or societal. Beckett and Maynard (2011), for example, point to cultural difference which may result in one society's or community's values giving high priority to individualism and personal freedom where another may prioritize the family or community above the individual.

In deciding on our preferences in human activity we must therefore be able to call upon an information and attitude 'bank' which has developed within us over time and been shaped by our socialization, experiences, education and professional development. Our 'framework for thinking' or 'world view', as discussed earlier, becomes central to the process of recognizing, applying and evaluating espoused values at a personal and professional level. This 'bank' will be well formed but subject to being a little unstable (in the open minded and reflective) and always susceptible to further change and enhancement in the light of experience and learning. Whether we are aware of it or not it is this bank that we will call upon to guide us in how we ought to act when confronted by the many tasks and situations requiring decision making in social work practice. We could argue for a pragmatic approach simply determining action on the basis of consequences but this would not reflect the reality as Beckett and Maynard (2011: 130) state: 'simply knowing the consequences will not help us to choose unless we have some means of determining which set of consequences is preferable'. It is only in the application of values to this equation that the choice of action can be taken. It is on this basis that principles of action such as 'least harm' or 'social justice' are built. These are expressions of preferred consequences based on beliefs about what is right and what is not.

This operation of values, I would suggest, comprises three parts: the belief (thought), the statement (word) and the behaviour (action). These are in a dynamic which can be stable (consistent with each other) or unstable (two or more in contradiction to each other). I might believe that it is wrong to inflict pain on another human being for the purpose of controlling them and then find myself stating that it is acceptable for a parent to slap a child for the purposes of behaviour management and not realize the contradiction until someone points it out to me. This also opens up for us the complexity of values once they are translated into action, as qualifications to our stated beliefs enter the scenario. It might be that an individual wishes to endure a certain level of pain or discomfort in order to achieve a behaviour change such as in some treatments for addictive behaviours. Should our baseline belief allow for flexibility of response?

For Rokeach (1973: 5) values are beliefs, offering the definition, 'A value is an enduring belief that a specific mode of conduct or end-state of existence is personally or socially preferable to an opposite or converse mode of conduct or end-state of existence.' This may be the case but a lot rests on the validity of the idea of an 'enduring belief' as this tends to ignore the multi-layered nature of the relationship between belief and conduct in values. It would be a mistake to disallow the propensity for values to be modified either in an evolutionary process or by a quite sudden event. The latter can be exemplified by the hurried politicization of groups and communities who have been on the receiving end of the consequences of government economic policy or the repressive state forces when challenging these consequences. Women in mining communities in the 1980s or young black people in deprived city areas in the post-war decades are two examples which readily come to mind. Both groups may well have started out believing, unquestioningly, in the importance of trusting the motives and purpose of institutions of society such as the police and government, only to have their views seriously challenged by events.

A very different definition of values is given by Clark (2000: 27) who states, 'They are constructs attributed by observers that have to be inferred by asking people questions about their attitudes and beliefs, and observing their utterances and behaviour in relation to areas of life where value issues are thought to be significant.' This signals the three elements or parts referred to earlier and allows for an absence of 'steady state' to be attributed to the nature of values. It also argues that values are the creation of the observer and therefore have no independent existence nor are they intrinsic to the individual.

Such analysis can lead us to highly interesting conceptual debates about the meaning, nature and language of values but will offer us little in the search for concrete guidance on what it is we are trying to achieve as professional social workers. It might be appropriate, here, to turn to Neil Thompson (2005) who summarizes the 'what are values' question by claiming them to be things which we consider to be important and that should be kept safe. He sees them as concrete and not just as abstract concepts because they 'have a very strong influence over what happens' and 'they will have a bearing on the decisions we make and the steps that we take regardless of our degree of open awareness of them' (p. 109). He continues to make the important point that the more we are aware of what our own values are the more likely it is that our actions will be consistent with our beliefs.

In what ways are values different to ethics? They certainly go together in social work practice yet a clear distinction between the two is not easy to establish other than the recognition of 'ethics' as an area of philosophical study, a subject in its own right (Clark 2000). For Dubois and Miley (2005) values are those things that people hold to be good and ethics is about what people think to be right. If we take from this that values relate to action (behaviour) and ethics to thought (belief) then this might help in distinguishing them as two parts of a single concept. Hugman's (2011: 136) alternative distinction suggests that ethics 'considers the formation and operation of moral values'. In other words ethics provides the operational application of values through setting out for us what is good or right in behaviour on the one hand and what is bad or wrong on the other. In separating out 'right' and 'good' we can begin to enlighten ourselves as to whether doing something is morally correct for the intrinsic value of the action or for the consequences it produces. We can do something simply because we believe it is right to do it or because we think the outcome will be beneficial. In the next section I will discuss how the dimensions of 'good' and 'right' are central to theoretical ideas on values and ethics.

This enables us to see values as the base material from which codes of behaviour (ethical statements) are derived. Terry (2007) suggests that while values have a personal quality as they arise from our own personal biographies, ethics translates values into professional and philosophical contexts. It follows that ethics gives the employee an external reference point of assumed shared approaches within a profession. Clark (2000) claims that values, as the base material for social work activity, should be few in number. These can then be employed as fundamental principles underlying the general social work aims of reducing harm and increasing benefit to human beings. He lists four principles: 'the worth and uniqueness of every person', 'the entitlement to justice', 'the aspiration to freedom' and 'the essentials of community'.

It is not my intention here to discuss these individually but rather to emphasize the point that this tends to confirm the limited use of identifying values in clarifying what would constitute good or desirable practice in social work. It is difficult to conceive of a situation in which anybody, from whatever political, religious or professional persuasion, would decline to sign up to Clark's value principles as the basis of their approach to life and other people. We nonetheless know that some of these same people will act in many different ways which will include oppression, abuse, discrimination, exclusion and impoverishment whether individually, collaboratively and institutionally. It is no surprise that statements of values within, between or outside professions show little difference.

Codes of ethics enable more effective consideration of behaviour as they outline in much more detail and more numerously how the professional is expected to behave and this allows a more effective way of measuring whether someone is doing 'right' or 'wrong'. They are, however, similarly vulnerable to having limited effect in assessing the impact of social work on the processes resulting in people finding themselves as service users. They operate as part of the professional structure and therefore focus on the activity of individuals employed by the profession to a greater extent than they do on the activity of the profession itself.

The focus of attention is more fruitfully turned to evaluating the consequences of actions which are carried out in the name of values. It is insufficient to simply claim respect for individuals or adherence to anti-oppressive practice. The activity of social work (not just the actions of individual social workers) is not always consistent with its value-based intentions because these are open to interpretation and analysis not least in terms of the perspective or 'world view' adopted by the individual worker. It is in the arena of practical interpretation of stated professional values that the distinction between personal and professional values becomes important as we have seen from the student social worker example earlier. Possession of a matured 'world view' equips us with a tool to evaluate not only our own actions but also the stated professional values and how they are operated. Only in this way can social workers legitimately question and challenge the institution of social work itself and its claim to possess and apply appropriate values and ethics. It is nonetheless a two-way process as professional ethical codes can and do lead to the challenging of personal values in practice in many areas, for example, abortion, adoption, safeguarding and behaviour management. The danger is that the application of codes of conduct may result in a focus on individual misdemeanour and avoidance of organizational and institutional wrongdoing.

Lists, codes and statements

It is generally assumed, although disputed, that a necessary trait of being a profession is the existence of a code of ethics outlining the conduct expected of its members (Banks 2006). A Code of Practice for Social Care Workers, including social workers was launched in the UK in September 2002 as required by the Care Standards Act 2000. The General Social Care Council (GSCC) made it clear that an employer could refer a social worker on the basis of concern which could result in the removal of registration for that individual therefore preventing them from holding the title 'social worker', a legally protected title since 1 April 2005. The standards are now set out by the Health and Care Professions Council, from 1st August 2012, as the 'Standards of Conduct, Performance and Ethics'. These are specifically geared towards the practice of individual professionals but deliberately do not offer specific guidance on how to behave in any particular situation. Apart from anything else this would be logistically impossible.

The 'listing' approach exemplified by the Code of Practice (GSCC 2010) is a development from earlier attempts to set out the values which should pertain to social work practice. Perhaps the most well known proponent, historically, is Biestek (1961) who set out his values for social work based on his Christian theological beliefs. This rendered the code, in effect, absolute and beyond question or challenge. His principle values included confidentiality, being non-judgemental, client self-determination and individualization. These are, of course, 'woolly' or vague terms which escape behavioural definition yet persist as virtues to be adhered to in day-to-day practice and can be found, albeit in alternative wording, in the current code of practice. The latter, unlike Biestek's proclamation, is derived from wide consultation with the various players in the social work sphere. Does this make it even less open to challenge while still being subject to the uncertainty of interpretation and yet used increasingly year on year to discipline and control the social work workforce? This is not to deny the need to prevent or punish obvious cases of abusive or harmful behaviour to service users but the use of listed codes of conduct must not divert attention away from analysis of the interpretation of these and the wider challenging and reform of the role, purpose and impact of social work in society, which is just as much a subject relevant to the values debate.

Shardlow (2009) sets out the limitation of the list approach citing how its development has resulted in several similar professional codes which have appeared through the British Association of Social Workers, the International Federation of Social Workers and the National Association of Social Workers (USA). He contends that the content of codes is too general in nature and that the codes more readily serve to provide professional identity for national and international organizations rather than providing clear guidance and assistance to the worker in deciding how to behave in particular situations.

The fact that social work now has an established code of conduct with regulation should not be taken as the definitive guide providing the answers to the less tangible and muddled questions which working with people throws up. Its focus, in practice, on the behaviour of individuals, and to a lesser extent, organizations does little to advance the main tenets of the often stated ethical aim of social justice. It is not easy to identify or measure the positive impact of existing codes and regulation at a wider social level on say, promoting fair access to and distribution of resources, equal treatment without prejudice or discrimination, reducing disadvantage and exclusion and challenging the abuse of power (see BASW 2011). Social work as a profession needs external reference points in order to be more effectively heard in national and international debates. As Whittington and Whittington (2007: 95) observe 'Yet social work's influence, as a distinctive lobby, has been simultaneously curtailed by social work's assimilation as an object of policy and regulation into the wider domain of social care and by the incorporation of social care codes and practice into government-endorsed systems of governance.' Finding the independent voice which helps realize the potential for political and social influence is a considerable challenge requiring a more panoramic field of attention not afforded by the current detail of ethical codes and individualized practice of regulation. I will return to this matter in considering questions of equality and social justice.

The application, use and focus of existing codes in the context of global capitalism and the prevailing political ideology explored in Chapter 2 offers some insight into the processes which reinforce the diversion away from matters of inequality, poverty and social justice. The combination of market-based service delivery, business models and managerialism derived from neo-liberal governance has lead to an increase in de-professionalized fear-based performance. With decades of government policies aimed at low taxation and restricted public sector spending social workers find themselves with increasing workloads and reduced resources, rigidly applying eligibility criteria and experiencing the dominance of surveillance and accountability over support and professional supervision. The propensity for error and omission in practice is greater and the energy of codes of practice is inevitably channelled towards individual fault and blame.

The conventional

The two major philosophical concepts which provide the basis for virtually all social work ethics are deontology and teleology (Hugman 2011). In exploring ethics the former is concerned with duty and rules of behaviour derived from what is right whereas the latter redirects us to the consequences of action for moral guidance. The deontological approach is most commonly associated with the work of Immanuel Kant. He was concerned with moral absolutes; that is, determining what is morally correct in dealing with other human beings and ourselves together with identifying what is right and what is wrong in terms of our moral duty to ourselves and others.

Respect for other people is based on the idea that each of us is a rational being capable of self-determination and therefore has desires and can make choices. This presents us with the maxim that we should never use others for our own ends as we would not welcome being used by others for purposes which ignored our own wishes in the process. Kant proposes that this kind of morality, at the base of which is respect, is intrinsic to all rational beings. As morality is derived from human reason then all moral judgements of right and wrong will be consistent and universal (Banks 2006). Kant's morality is framed within the idea of the 'categorical imperative' which means that there is no room for negotiation or interpretation when it comes to universalized statements of what is right and wrong. The 'categorical imperative' is the unconditional order or command we must all follow in our interactions and attitude towards others and ourselves. This is the control on our tendency to act in immoral ways derived from being natural animals. Behaving morally becomes a duty and our reason tells us how we ought to act.

Smith (2008a) argues that, contrary to this, there has to be the facility to determine whether and how one does something based on the circumstances involved. He gives the example of suicide grounded in self-love, which Kant argues cannot be a universal maxim as it contradicts preservation based on self-love. Smith claims, persuasively, that self-love can promote both preservation and suicide if the latter is voluntary and does not harm others. People with degenerative terminal conditions may wish to end their lives at a certain point out of self-love as expressed in wishing to maintain dignity and awareness and to avoid personal suffering.

For Kant, acting in a right way is not something we achieve by reference to external rules or guidance but rather an autonomous, self-governed element of human behaviour (Smith 2008a). This helps in understanding the similarity between different professional codes of practice as these, in deontological terms, are the externalized expression of morality intrinsic to humankind. As we have seen this is not without its potential contradictions and will not resolve all our practice dilemmas. We are commanded to act morally on the basis that all humans possess reason/rationality and are therefore never just a means to another's end but an end themselves. Then what are we to do in respect of those who lack reason or rationality, for example very young children, those with failing mental capacity, serious mental health difficulties or learning disabilities? Kantian philosophy would have us believe that these people could be placed in the same category as non-rational animals and inanimate objects which he collectively groups as 'things' (Heath 1997). In other words, such people could be used as a means to achieve the aims of others. The many cases of abuse of service users highlight the manner in which some professionals have acted according to this personal moral code, seeing these groups as either not fully formed humans (children) or as less than fully human. It also brings into focus debates about how we should view and treat certain groups in society such as children when issues of control, punishment and exploitation come to the fore. This dichotomy can only be resolved by classifying only inanimate objects as 'things' and asserting the equal value of all human beings for their own sake as human beings. Many might argue that non-human animals should also be excluded from being classified as 'things' but this is a topic for discussion elsewhere.

As Banks (2006) has said Kantian ethics is at the root of much of social work's stated ethics as exemplified in Biestek's (1961) casework principles and in the several ethical codes which have followed on from these. The essentials of respect for the individual and self-determination have been the bedrock of practice for several decades now and therein resides a further problem. Apart from leaving the practitioner with ill-defined terms such as respect and self-determination the singularity of attention to the personal relationship of one-to-one work does not reflect the reality of the professional role or predicament. Practitioners work in organizations with mission statements, rules and goals and are subject to the strictures of changeable social policy and legislation. Concentration on the personal relationship also fails to accommodate all the stated aims of social work which include the aspiration to work towards social justice. There is a need to seek other perspectives and theories on ethics. The seemingly universal foundation for professional ethics offered by Kantian philosophy and translated as respect for individuals has taken on 'the character of indispensability' (Clark 2000). In showing a preference for a pluralist approach he goes on to suggest that 'The status of indispensible principles is understood to be dominant until proved otherwise, ... no single theory is comprehensive or persuasive enough to earn the comprehensive defeat of all its rivals' (p. 67).

Teleological theory instructs us that what is right is that which results in the greatest good. In other words, actions whose consequences result in maximizing good experiences for the greatest number of people are morally correct or right. The most influential teleological theory is 'Utilitarianism' as espoused by Jeremy Bentham (1948) in his work *The Principles of Morals and Legislation*. This, however, allows for a rather wide-ranging and ultimately unhelpful meaning of good. In an attempt to answer this problem and referring to utilitarianism as a version of 'consequentialism', Terry (2007) points out that John Stuart Mill developed the concept so that good moral decisions where those that furthered human welfare. This position allows for an acknowledgement that individual work with service users can promote human welfare but also enables a much greater level of judgement to be made on the assessment of circumstances and outcomes than is achievable in Kantian ethics and moves us on from the personal to the social. For example decisions on exclusion and inclusion in respect of welfare services are allowable in the light of scarce resources and the aim of benefiting those in most need and the largest number possible. Teleological approaches also alert the individual professional to think of the consequences of their actions beyond the individual(s) they are working with at any one time. If workers are competing with each other for resources for their service users or implementing policies to restrict provision to certain groups in society then they can call themselves and others to account for actions which fail in or counteract the furthering of human welfare.

On the other hand, at a social and political level, this democratizing of determining what is good for as many as possible could lead to actions that result in the achievement of populist aims which run contrary to the assumed values of social work practice. For example the argument for discriminatory policies on the basis of racism, sexism or disablism would be acceptable if the majority felt strongly enough that they would benefit from such policies. The question of what is right is less important than what produces the most good and if the desire for discrimination is as strong in the majority as the desire to challenge it in the minority then discrimination by the majority becomes justified from a utilitarian standpoint.

The radical

The two giants of social work ethics, Kantian and Utilitarian approaches, have been the subject of much challenge from a range of perspectives from post-modern and structural schools of thought. These alternative approaches question the validity of a morality based on concepts of 'duty' or 'responsibility' framed in the language of directives and placed as an obligation on individuals. A morality born of people's natural humanity or social inclination provides a greater opportunity for human ethical action to arise from the self and collectively in terms of personal qualities and beliefs about the dynamics of the social world. This also nurtures a capacity to challenge the dictates of duties, codes and responsibilities through a process of experimentation and reflection in dealing with the complexities of the human condition.

A counter to 'the ends justify the means' maxim of utilitarianism can be found in the application of 'discourse ethics' (Habermas 1992). For Habermas moral decisions can only ever be derived from open communication leading to true consensus. All those likely to be affected by the decision must be involved and equality of contribution must apply to all those competent to contribute. Each must seek empathic understanding of the others' position and agreement reached only when all accept the consequences of the decision (Houston 2010). This provides a clear defence for the meaningful inclusion of service users in decision making processes in all situations while highlighting the way in which such inclusion should be structured and operated. The process fosters the accommodation of diversity of thinking and values as well as the establishment of a single 'right' approach as the consensus decision is taken to be 'that one moral view ... justified above all others' (Houston 2010: 100).

The complexity of involvement or participation is reflected in the sense of exclusion many service users experience despite being present in discussions and supported by professional staff. A student related this difficulty in reporting an incident where a mother expressed the feeling that she would be seen as blocking a school trying to meet the needs of her son if she offered her opinion on the recommendations of his teachers. In meetings she felt unable to contribute honestly and was intimidated by the number of teachers present. Achieving the necessary parameters of discourse ethics in such situations is immensely difficult. Habermas's principles of 'discourse ethics' become more of an ideal or aspiration when placed in the context of both micro and macro situations whether it be the case conference or the processes of exclusion and oppression in wider society. They nonetheless set a standard to be worked towards and against which practice can be measured, if we are to achieve ethical conduct at different levels. Discourse ethics also sends an important message to practitioners that it is legitimate to seek to have one's voice heard on an equal basis in the development of policy and practice and in decision making in organizational and political forums, and to challenge attempts to exclude, undermine or in other ways attack the professional workforce in the name of asserting hierarchical custom, management rights or political prerogative.

Post-modern theorists ask us to accept that striving for the universal truth of what is moral is a pointless task. The question of how we behave to each other is by definition a messy business as human beings and their behaviour are unpredictable. We might make grand statements about what our ethical standards and values are but they cannot account for nor predict how we will respond or react to others in the specifics of different situations. Bauman (1993) in proposing a form of post-modern ethics concluded that the individual is moral before the working out of what is moral behaviour or the creation of ethical codes. We are all confronted by uncertainty, ambivalence and insecurity in the face of encountering others. There are no easy, ordered answers to how to behave or what decisions to make; there is only the responsive morality of responsibility for others and this can lead to each of us being capable of and doing both good and bad. Morality comes from within so it is only through self-examination or being reflexive that we come to know our own morality rather than by reference to external benchmarks which we can often use as shields to hide behind or pin our self-righteousness to. The importance of the subjective in morality is highlighted in this particular perspective.

A similarly subjective but nurture- not nature-based proposition comes from 'virtue ethics' whereby the personality of the actor becomes the central source of moral or ethical behaviour (Clifford and Burke 2009). The consequences of actions are not the measure of morality but the intention of the individual as expressions of their character, virtuous or otherwise. The virtuous character will do things through intrinsic motivation, not in an attempt to abide by a set of regulations or procedures. Compassion, selflessness, honesty, caring and courage will be some of the guiding personality features associated with the virtuous person. Such aspects can be used to build a concept of the type of person who is suitable for certain professional roles such as social worker. By definition virtuous activity is a social activity as it is built on our interactions and communications with others. We need to learn about ourselves and our impact on others from these encounters. This can only happen if we engage in processes of reflection giving us deeper insights to what type of person we are and the content and validity of our claim to virtue. Being ethical becomes a developmental process and requires a commitment to changing through growing self-awareness. There is no checklist against which we can sign-off as a job well done. Gray and Webb (2010: 110) summarize thus: 'virtue ethics is the formation of a way of being developed through practice inside a culture of experience, reflection, understanding and judgement which brings its (virtuous) self into contact with others'. The subjective dimension to ethical practice is that invisible guardian repeatedly asking us to consider if, through our actions, we have done right by others, not just individually but also collectively. In a world of social division and exclusionary processes a social worker cannot act without impacting on both and both are of equal import in determining the virtue of our actions.

The second, yet equally salient, element in post-modern approaches to ethics and values is relativism. The starting point is that there is no universal objective morality as the only reality is the subjective experience of individuals. If we then recognize the diversity of human kind and the consequent difference in cultures across the globe then it follows that morality is necessarily relative to each culture (and individual) and that no one culture or individual can lay claim to superiority or rightness of morality or ethics. The problem with contesting this claim is that whereas one can often resolve differences in beliefs on facts by reference to some objective truth, in the world of moral relativism there is no objective reference point, only the construction of a consensus about what might be right or wrong. If there is a dispute about whether the world is flat or round we can now refer to evidence, including pictures from space, to settle such a dispute. Trying to settle the dispute between those who think that assisted suicide is wrong in all circumstances and those who think it is acceptable in some circumstances remains a matter of contested beliefs with no external objective reference point. Social workers face considerable difficulty in reconciling the celebration of diversity with the application of a defined value system in their day-to-day work. For the most part the professional can deploy the requirements of law in any particular situation to cut through the ethical debate but this usually adds to rather than takes away from the depth of the moral dilemma pertaining to any specific situation.

The adoption of a relativist stance could render social workers powerless in many situations in their attempts to justify, on ethical grounds, interventions designed to challenge what they saw as patriarchy, corporal punishment, physical mutilation, exploitation or abuse. If these are tolerated or promoted in certain cultures then how is anyone in a position to claim they are right or wrong? Smith (2008a: 133) retorts that relativist thinking and reasoning can nonetheless be critically analysed and 'thus some beliefs can be shown to be more or less reasonable than their rivals. Through this process, we can work towards the moral beliefs that are supported by the best reasons.' Interestingly the argument that moral relativism is a sound defence against cultural and moral imperialism should not lead to a denial of the existence of universal moral principles. By definition relativism precludes any one culture from espousing its own beliefs and practices as right other than within its own confines. This allows for the pursuit of what might be considered right, across cultures.

For the most part conventional perspectives on ethics are individualistic and seek to provide some guidance on how we should behave in our interactions with other individuals. While post-modern thinking radically challenges these objective attempts to define ethical behaviour they are very much rooted in the subjective world of the individual actor and reject the application of overarching processes which determine social, political and economic relations in society. The practitioner is left to act either by reason of obligation to external codes derived from externally constructed concepts of right or good or in accord with a commitment to working with diversity with no reference to a core set of beliefs. It follows that they are therefore likely to act, not by reference to reasoned conclusions on the right way to proceed based on a knowledge and understanding of social and interpersonal processes, but solely through the application of one or more of the law, organizational policies or professional codes.

There is an often ignored radical tradition in social work which has the potential to grant a moral perspective which would support workers developing a practice incorporating a 'world view'. In the 1960s and 1970s the emergence of radical social work (Lavalette 2011) promoted a re-thinking of the traditional practice of social work moving from the individualism of applied psychological theory to the structural influences detailed in sociological writings from Marxism, feminism and social constructionists. A recognition that marginalization, deprivation and disenfranchisement affected a diverse range of groups with different consequences and responses led to a break from the tenets of 1970s radical social work and saw the emergence of 'single issue' campaigns and literature from the 1980s onward. In parallel to this the ever-growing influence of anti-oppressive practice aimed to create a practice which drew on the commonality of individual social divisions. The principle values underpinning anti-oppressive practice are summarized by Dominelli (2010: 161) as 'the ideals of equality, egalitarian power relations, social justice, empowerment, human rights and citizenship'. The professional using an anti-oppressive approach is called upon to address the structural context of service users' situations.

This represents a re-assertion of social justice as an ethical aim and the adoption of collective activity as a positive professional response to social division. It is manifesting itself in increasing interest and participation in a current radical expression within social work. This is not only committed to anti-oppressive practice but to collaborative networking with a range of groups and organizations challenging the political and economic doctrines and practices which play a major part in determining the plight of the vast majority of service users. One of Baldwin's (2011: 204) conclusions for social workers is that 'We should get used to judging our own and our organisations' practice on the values of social justice, rather than the values of resource control, privatisation and profit. Our profession is here to make the social work – not the markets work.'

Social justice and equality

It has been clearly stated that social work is in part about social change and that seek-ing social justice is not contested. As we have seen such aspirations are written into the several professional codes. A colleague turned to me recently and expressed disap-pointment that little had been achieved in reducing inequalities in wealth, education and health in our country in the several decades both of us had been involved in social work despite the developments in social work training and the ever-increasing litera-ture on anti-oppressive, radical and critical practice and their attempts to highlight the structural context of work with service users.

The direction of practice is exclusively and incessantly towards work with indi-viduals and families, and while there is considerable need and scope for the effective application of anti-oppression to individual situations (Dominelli 2010) particularly through sensitivity to diversity and culture (Banks 2006) there is little evidence that this has any incremental impact on wider social injustices and inequalities. The work of students is now permeated by references to anti-oppressive approaches but rarely does the ethical aim of achieving social justice make an appearance in their written deliberations. In a reflection on the vision of social work, Chris Jones (2011: 42) lays claim to the potential of a resurgence in radical principles to reignite 'a social work that ... saw how rigorous and deep analysis of society and its dynamics could lead to forms of practice which strengthened rather than undermined people. It was a social work based on solidarities and alliances and ... offered ways of working that were far less likely to stigmatise and harm than is the case today.'

The pursuit of social justice as an ethical aim requires clarification of what is meant by social justice as it is, again, a goal appropriated by people holding a wide range of different positions politically and ideologically. As Clifford and Burke (2009) have pointed out, the ideas of social justice and equality are often criticized as products of and are therefore defined by the dominant economic system of modern capitalism and its allied social relations. It is not surprising that existing codes of ethics and conduct (with the exception of that of the International Federation of Social Work), which arise within this context incorporate the term social justice but give little substance to the significant social change required to achieve it. Reference to it, in large part, confines activity towards its realization to the individual interactions between social workers and their service users avoiding the difficult area of challenging structural, political, economic and institutional forces conspiring to diminish its meaning to merely 'equality of opportunity' in an unequal world.

If the ethical and moral basis of social work steers it to focus on helping people function to their own satisfaction on a day-to-day basis in the face of deprivation, loss, exclusion and oppression then it also has to be about addressing those factors which contribute to these situational determinants. One consequence of doing one without the other is that social workers become absorbed into competing with each other for resources for 'their' service users and thereby partake in a process of competitive exclusion which they would find difficult to defend on ethical and moral grounds beyond the principles of utilitarianism. This is a difficult dilemma as it would be highly problematic to claim that it would be acceptable to assert the abandonment of trying to resolve individual difficulties in the short term for the realization of broader positive social change in the future. Banks (2006) alerts us to this criticism of proponents of radical social work and it could be argued that sacrificing those living in crisis now for a better life for all later would be tantamount to ideological tyranny. To fail to properly address the wider sources of the immediate situational problems for individuals, on the other hand, contains the danger that the worker becomes part of the problem for service users as a whole, now and in the future, rather than part of the solution. An uncomfortable alliance between conventional individual approaches paralleled with action for social change may be that which is demanded by an ethically valid social work which incorporates social justice as a radical aim.

The uniqueness and primacy afforded each individual human being in social work implies that underpinning the social work view is the idea of a society of equals which is consistent with the proclamations of all moral perspectives in one form or another. It follows that individuals in society should be treated equally in terms of respect, liberties, rights and opportunities. This should be reflected in the way society distributes its resources so that inequality in income and wealth is minimized. For those of a right-wing free market orientation equality to act freely and voluntarily while protected from coercion and theft is sufficient to achieve social justice. In practice what we see is significant and increasing inequalities in income, wealth, influence and opportunity resulting from such an arrangement. Nozick (2001) argues that this is acceptable as it is not how much you accumulate that matters; it is how you accumulate it that makes the process just or not. This is seen as unjust to those of a more social and democratic persuasion who espouse equal treatment through equality of opportunity.

Genuine equality of opportunity is an essential principle of social justice in terms of inequalities in income and wealth according to Rawls (2005). This does not preclude the existence of economic inequalities so long as they arise from equality of opportunity to acquire position and that they bestow greatest benefit on the least well off. The latter is Rawls's difference principle which defines the only condition under which inequality can exist. His principle of equal basic rights and liberties, including equality of opportunity, takes priority in all circumstances. The collective good is not of concern although equality among individuals is highlighted and the exploitation of the less well off by the well off is disallowed. Cooperation between people comes from mutual respect. For equality of opportunity to be fair then all have to have an equal chance of achieving positions aspired for based on their talent and motivation. Yet this still leaves a lot to luck as we cannot control what talents we are born with, who our parents are, our relative economic position, our educational opportunities, etc. Rawls therefore argues that inequality is acceptable to the degree that those who benefit have the fruits of their advantage used to improve the lot of those less well off. Increases in wealth, in this way, provide greater overall wealth for distribution. The necessary principle is that no one gains advantage at the expense of someone else with the welfare state, universal education and health provision, social security and progressive taxation being the mechanisms which ensure this happens.

The principles set out above suggest that social justice is derived from a compromise between the freedom of the market and the need to manage it in such a way that no one suffers unduly as a result of factors beyond their control. The acts of individuals in pursuing greater wealth are not constrained on any personal moral grounds but only through societal institutions and government making decisions about what are allowable differences in income and wealth within the limits of public acceptability. Those seeking a more egalitarian approach would argue that the personal pursuit of wealth invariably leads to the less well off being relatively worse off and that this exacerbates inequalities in all areas of social and individual life. The difference principle does not address this sufficiently to ensure true justice. Cohen (2008) argues that principles of action to achieve greater equality should apply at both the institutional and the individual level. The 'reasonable' inequality of Rawls's social justice is contradicted by the acquisitiveness of individuals in the free market maximizing the advantage granted them by luck or chance. Where there is inequality of condition resulting from the unfair distribution of resources, wealth and income (Smith 2008a) then it is not possible to have fair equality of opportunity. Even if equality of opportunity were achieved it would not necessarily result in social justice. Equality of opportunity only provides for individuals to avail themselves of the means to improve their personal lot. It does not address the structural divisions between rich and poor and the personal and inter-personal psychological, emotional and health problems which result from the associated stigmatization, prejudice, unequal relationships and power differentials which permeate society. Such divisions further draw resources away from the needs of the less well off, whose position social workers strive to improve. Without turning to the question of inequality of condition as a focus of attention social work can only fail in one of its core ethical aims. As Smith (2008a) suggests, 'social justice requires not only equality of civil and political rights and fair equality of opportunity, but also equality of condition'.

Key points

1 Values represent a complexity and depth of human thought and action which is ill served by shallow assertions of one's moral position.
2 Knowledge and understanding of our own values requires us to explore the personal and social context of our own experience and its relationship to the store of views and attitudes which we call upon in practice.
3 Values are belief-based preferences which can change with experience and reflection.
4 Ethics may be seen as the formal study and external representation of personal values.
5 Value statements offer little practical guidance as they are open to wide interpretation when applied.

6 Professional ethical codes should be challenged critically in the context of an unequal and unjust society.
7 Consideration of social justice is a neglected area of social work values and ethics.
8 Addressing issues of inequality is central to the realization of the purpose of social work.

Questions for discussion

1 Is a commitment to social justice through equality of condition compatible with stated social work values?
2 Consider instances where personal ethical codes conflict with the professional ethical codes and discuss the implications.
3 How might you apply the principles of discourse ethics in your practice with service users, as an employee and in multi-professional activity?

4 Power in social work

'It seems to me that all human experience is inextricably tied to feelings of power and control over one's life, which in turn are connected to actual circumstances'

(Hearn 2012: 3)

Power plays a significant part in all human relationships at all levels in society. The ability of individuals and institutions to control, oppress and exploit others or to enable, empower and emancipate is largely determined by differentials in the possession and use of power. Inequalities through class, race, gender, age, sexuality and ability are all mediated by the social relations characterized by relative positions of power in society. Being of a particular ethnic origin, for example, might make it more difficult for you to exercise control over what happens to you in your daily life if you are subject to racial abuse or denied access to opportunities because of your ethnicity.

Although everywhere, power is not something we can see or touch. It is a social concept which we evidence through its impact on people and their attempts to acquire and apply it in everyday activity. It is both a part of human interaction whereby one or more people have or gain control over others and a personal possession through which one gains or loses control over one's own life. The possession and use of power is inextricably linked to the value base and ethical position which social workers adopt in their practice and cannot be considered without reference back to these in our reflection on our actions.

Michael Foucault (2006) directs us to an example of a clear imbalance of power in which power flows only in one direction. This is exemplified, in cases cited by him, by the power of the doctor over patient in mental health treatment in France in the nineteenth century. An initial show of force is used to make it clear that there is no exchange or reciprocity available or allowed in the meeting of doctor and patient. Such absolutely statutory difference of level in the possession, application and process of power is thought to be less evident in modern industrial democratic societies but the grounds for its existence can still be observed in the social, economic and political relations of these same societies. Expositions of the unseemly entanglement of politicians, the press and the police in the 'phone hacking' scandal in the UK in 2011 stand as testimony to the manner in which collaboration in the pursuit and retention of power can lay bare the fragility of the heralded democracy of modern western nations. Also on a micro level, in social work, the danger of more obvious power differentials needs to be acknowledged and explored to ensure that the potential for this imbalance to be present in any working relationships is minimized and any difference made transparent in the communication between professional and service user.

Power in social work activity is of particular import as the starting point for most service users is disadvantage, social exclusion and poverty. The situational position of the social work service user within the professional relationship is one of deprivation. This deprivation gives rise to need and the service user therefore seeks or is directed to have these needs met and the deprivation removed by those who possess the resources to enable this. If the state of deprivation becomes an almost permanent state as a result of structural processes such as government policy and economic and social inequalities and oppressions then the service user remains always in a condition of need. In this way the service user is permanently in a relative position whereby they lack the resources necessary to gain power and thereby control over their predicament. Release from this position of disadvantage has to be purchased through achieving prescribed changes in behaviour within a process of professional surveillance and discretion, which may or may not involve varying degrees of personal empowerment and choice on the part of the service user. If the service user thinks of or perceives the social worker to be part of the 'system' of institutions and regulations which perpetuate deprivation and oppression then it becomes even harder for the professional to reduce the discrepancy in power. The thinking social worker will be conscious of such differentials in working with service users. The aim is to attempt to achieve a professional relationship in which there is a two-way process with clear dialogue and in which power factors undermining this are minimized.

Of course power relations are complex so the avenue for exploring and influencing the dynamics involved is open to those with the motivation and insight to take advantage of this, whether they be the service user seeking greater control over their situation or the professional seeking to realize meaningful outcomes of a measurable anti-oppressive nature. Being able to demonstrate that anti-oppression is taking place involves the service user actually acquiring the means to positively use power and control as an outcome of social work intervention. How the worker conducts themselves in the process of their interactions with the service user is important but not sufficient on its own. This warning is given by Wilson and Beresford (2000: 553) in referring to 'the failure so far to address the use of social work and social care services as an area of difference and category of social division'. They warn that the process of applying anti-oppressive practice in itself as a feature of good social work practice might well result in the appropriation of anti-oppression by the profession and thereby exacerbate the power differential between practitioner and user. Anti-oppression for Wilson and Beresford has to be rooted in the thinking and activity of service users as the primary source of resistance and change. Such apparent dichotomies are picked up by Smith (2008b: 3) who suggests in his detailed analysis of power and social work that 'The paradoxical and multifaceted nature of social work's relationship to power, and its power relationships, clearly represent a significant challenge.'

The social worker's power is conferred by several institutional variants including the organizational context, professional status, legal authority, academic and vocational qualification, language, knowledge, class, social legitimacy, the state and the 'office' as the professional base. This can result in a ritual imbalance of power when professional intervention occurs, at least from the point of view of the service user. By connecting the social work relationship with the dimensions of power identified and explored by French and Raven (1959) we can outline the different ways in which a service user might experience social work involvement. They may see the social worker as someone to defer to (referent power) or as someone who holds the key to resources (reward power); perhaps as an expert (expert power) or in a position to withhold, deprive and punish (coercive power) or as possessing legitimate authority (legitimate power). The relative position and different perceptions of those involved clearly becomes important here. We can add to this the language of discipline and order, derived from legal, organizational and scientific mandates, which the professional is constrained to use. From this a model of acquiescent obedience is presented to the recipients of service for them to follow. Service users begin from a state of power deficit as they struggle to retain control over their lives and circumstances. Social workers have to be keenly aware that their actions can either help people gain more control or undermine their efforts and further disempower them. Moving from the interpersonal level to the experience of working in organizations, social workers are subject to power differentials which have been exacerbated by changes in working arrangements and relationship structures over recent decades and at the socio-political level social workers' activities are further framed within the relationship between the state, the economic system and the social work service. These different levels of contexts of power are worthy of equal consideration as it is within these that the constraints on the power of the professional and therefore their ability to empower service users are directly influenced by several different forces.

The nature of power

The complexity of power as an interactive process is emphasized by Gilbert and Powell (2010: 6) in referring to Foucault's outline of its omnipresence: 'Foucault rejects claims that any particular group or class have a monopoly over power rather, power circulates via a myriad of social networks penetrating deep into the far corners of social life playing out its effects through the everyday interactions of autonomous individuals.' This moves us from the idea of power being a linear process of domination and control to it being 'relational'. As Veyne (2010: 94) says, power 'is the most common and everyday thing and is to be found everywhere. There is power at work in a family, between two lovers, in the workshop and in one-way streets. Millions of little powers form the weft of society in which individuals constitute the warp.' Verne goes on to claim that as there is power everywhere then there is liberty everywhere. In the field of social work this has to be tempered by the possibility of power appearing to operate in a linear fashion in many circumstances where the balance of power is clearly skewed in favour of a particular party. The power of a child is effectively stripped away when they find themselves being abused by an adult where the representatives of authority inadvertently collude with the abuser by failing to address the child directly or to communicate effectively with others in possession of some knowledge of the situation. In this case it appears that the child is not in anyway acquiescing in the abuse but the facility to abuse might be enhanced by the child's own sense of guilt, fear or responsibility, however devoid of stability relationships may be. The crucial positioning of the professional as a source of power for the child to be able to resist against the abuse in such situations hardly needs spelling out here but failings of communication are repeatedly identified in the numerous serious case reviews which follow incidents of significant harm or death (Brandon et al. 2009).

If we accept that power is relational then in all circumstances of social work intervention there is the potential to change or modify these relations. Such analysis might provide a positive perspective on the potential for change towards a more even distribution of power in individual relationships or between certain groups but falls short in other respects. Taking the omnipresent/relational view of power in theoretical isolation does present us with some problems. In moving from overarching, 'grand' views of society these post-modern/post-structural ideas reject any suggestion that it is any longer possible to make sense of the world or society as a whole, whether this be in terms of power or other social processes. Identity and diversity become the hinterland for exploring the nature and causes of oppression. As Ferguson and Lavalette (2004: 298) claim 'postmodern or post-structuralist approaches, [are] fiercely hostile to any attempt to make sense of the world as a totality'. They further argue that these approaches have laid claim to the radical arm of social work and yet point to evidence suggesting that most people's sense of powerlessness is derived from dispossession and marginalization as products of the economic and political systems directing their lives.

In a broader social sense the many forces in society which operate to instil the desire for social order may well produce an internalized apathy/acceptance in people allowing for their oppression and control with little questioning or resistance. This submission to the ways ascribed to us by others may well become weaved into the tapestry of our identities allowing us to locate ourselves in the 'acceptable', socially valued group (Lukes 2005). The discourse on how we should behave and what we might consider deviant is mediated through family, schools, religion and the workplace so we develop a strong element of self control modelled on the preferences of the dominant order of the time. In the view of Althusser (1977) these social institutions act as the 'ideological apparatus' of the state in ensuring adherence to particular codes of behaviour, which bolster the dominant system and enable the maintenance of the status quo. The expertise of the professional becomes a key ally of government, albeit with semi-autonomous status, in regulating the choices and behaviours of those they come into contact with. 'Professionals are both the instrument and the subject of government, the governor and the governed' (Fournier 1999: 285).

The manner in which this operates can range from the use of force, as might be adopted in applying the law in child safeguarding and mental health cases, through to manipulation in leading someone to a situation they cannot retreat from easily. I was recently informed of social workers using the 'Facebook' social networking site as a matter of routine to locate absconding young people and then to persuade them into meeting, which ultimately led to their return to their required place of residence. For the social workers involved this was an effective way of securing a place of safety for those they believed to be highly vulnerable. While the intent to achieve this end might not in itself be questioned, the value base informing the process or means adopted could at least be subject to challenge. Are the social workers involved using persuasion or deception as a form of manipulation which lacks a certain level of honesty and openness? Coercing someone into making a choice they might at first resist is another means of using power through offering, directly or indirectly, a range of alternatives which renders the selection of the professional's preferred or only available option the only reasonable outcome from the service user's perspective. For example, an older person might accept a package of care they feel is less than adequate, withdrawing their initial resistance, as they fear that more damaging deprivation might follow from persisting to challenge what is on offer.

Closely allied to manipulation is influence, a process of power which can be automatically applied almost without knowledge of the perpetrator. I have often been surprised by colleagues who point out to me the influence the words or presence of certain individuals have just by virtue of who they are or how they are perceived. When not intentionally claiming authority we might not realize the influence we can have over others or the power of our words if we are unaware of how others see or respond to us. This could be construed as a form of 'charisma' (Weber 1992) but not necessarily derived from the possession of any superhuman qualities or the bestowal of divine powers. It is most definitely to do with how our words, behaviours and presence are received by others. The propensity for our influence over others to be evidenced is magnified in the context of the professional/ service user relationship for reasons of existing power differentials highlighted earlier.

Authority, as another form of power, can be conferred on someone by the allocation of position, the possession of legal powers, the attributes of a title or the participation of all in the social framework of hierarchy which permeates modern living. Authority can be legitimate in being accepted by the majority or illegitimate in not having popular support but being maintained through force. Attempts by governments to maintain authority in the face of evidently unpopular policies are manifest in the use of the police or armed forces to control and undermine opposition under the guise of defending democracy. This has been clearly demonstrated in the UK where, following the 2010 General Election, a coalition government was formed as no one political party gained a sufficient majority of parliamentary seats. Although constitutionally legitimate the government proceeded to introduce major reforms to the NHS, education and the public sector without any clear democratic mandate for these specific policies. The subsequent unrest and protest have been met with police practices such as the 'kettling' of young people and others and prosecution policies which have been questioned and challenged from different sectors of society for their haste and severity. These methods have been referred to by Althusser (1977) and others as 'repressive state apparatuses'.

The fact that people protest or challenge demonstrates that it does not follow that social forces 'determine' the responses of either the service user or the professional, rather people might recognize these forces as 'obstacles' against which they can react either in thought or action or both (Foucault 2001). This includes being able to critically understand the knowledge base of social work and how it is created in a particular time and place under the influence of the forces of social order. Increasingly such knowledge derives its power and legitimacy from being grounded in scientific study which implies some objective neutrality. In other words, because knowledge is science based it is claimed it is not tainted by the same social forces that human beings are. It is clear, however, that scientific study is undertaken by human beings at particular times in history and in particular geographical and cultural locations therefore its outcomes cannot necessarily claim any such neutrality or legitimacy simply on the basis that it is called scientific. The importation from the USA of 'brief therapy', for example, as an effective evidence-based intervention for helping people change cannot be separated out from the need for insurance companies in the USA to keep costs to a minimum and from the model this provides for governments in the UK to reduce public spending and seek privatization alternatives to public services.

For Foucault the social forces which are at play at any time form the discourse, or social creation, which sets the framework of behaviour, meanings, attitudes and values which we either acquiesce in or challenge. Veyne (2010) refers to this as the 'discursive fishbowl' which an individual can either remain trapped inside or be freed from to discover their own creative or critical thought and action. Only through escape from the 'discursive fishbowl' can the dominant discourse be identified, directly challenged and the potential to de-assemble the framework established by such dominance be realized.

Social work is a part of the dialectic process in society (Giddens 1984) in which control and resistance are in continual opposition producing a variety of outcomes and through which the oppressed or dependent can influence the actions of those who dominate. In a society of extreme inequalities it is a basic requirement of caring professionals to operate outside the 'discursive fishbowl' and continually question their own practices and the detail of social and economic policy which directly impact on the lives of users of services. Being 'aware' in this way as a necessary pre-requisite to good practice is effectively outlined by Blok (2012: 122):

> From a social-critical point of view, association and connection with the less powerful people in society is needed to stimulate more social justice in society. Power is an important factor for functioning and success within society. Social awareness and dialectic thinking are key in the explanation of human behavior. The relation between 'being' and 'awareness' is crucial in critical analysis of social developments.

Power in organizations

In speaking with a recently retired social work manager and academic, who had returned to part-time practice, he observed that

> Working recently in a child care team of a local authority I was dismayed at the practice. The social workers were very distant from the parents. They did what they had to do to secure the safeguarding of children at the expense of working with parents. There was no resource, either time or energy put into working to assess and support the potential of parents to parent. In their dealings with service users they replicated the managerial approach which they themselves were subject to.

This can manifest itself in a reluctance or inability to communicate in an open, detailed and inclusive way through face-to-face contact which might allow people to better understand the predicament they find themselves in and the procedures and processes to which they have become subjected. Letters and even emails might be exchanged but service users' attempts to enter into face-to-face communication can be then interpreted as pestering or persistence with consequent admonishment from managers and dismissal or exclusion from the organization. In this way the service provider fails to learn anything from the service user, disempowers them and confirms the rightness of its own approach.

Fook (2002) suggests that the uncertainty and creativity present in the postmodern age gives social work the opportunity to show a positive appreciation and facilitation of service users creating and exercising their own power. The example above indicates the difficulty facing social workers in aspiring to this goal. If problems are narrowly constructed and needs similarly defined in the absence of concepts of creative and collective responses then professional practice with increased individual accountability and standardization is likely to operate in a controlling environment within a culture of blame, rigid procedure and fear (Gilbert and Powell 2010). Professionals should be accountable and best practice should be shared across geographical and professional boundaries but not at the cost of loss of creative engagement with service users which could offer a route to acknowledging and championing the value of both the service users' and social workers' knowledges.

Gilbert and Powell go on to cite Scheyett (2006) in his consideration of how knowledge and power are affected by the promotion of evidence-based practice and organizational preference for this approach:

> Discourses of evidence based practice effectively silence both the service user and the practitioner. This occurs as the dialogue between service users and practitioners over experiences and knowledge of the 'real world' become subjugated to disciplinary knowledge external to this dialogue which, through its status as truth, discredits alternative conceptions of events and their meanings.
> (Gilbert and Powell 2010: 13)

This is arguing that, in effect, any opportunity to develop knowledge and theory from the everyday interactions of worker and service user are rejected as illegitimate and insufficiently scientific and measurable. The service users become objectified as documented items of information which can be measured, calculated and differentiated for the purpose of applying evidence-based practice. Smith (2008b) summarizes a complementary process arising from the valuing of management in organizations over professional practice. Over time, the space available for independent thought, decision making and action on the part of the practitioner has been progressively reduced by the belief in and imposition of what amounts to technical approaches to the complexity of problems in living.

The discrediting of professional practitioner knowledge is part of a wider process of de-professionalization through which the control of professionals becomes more manifest. Professional autonomy is still implied by the conferment of public and legal status by, for example, the creation of the protected title of 'social worker' in the UK. This protection means that only those with a recognized academic qualification and registration with the relevant statutory body (the GSCC as at 2011) can call themselves social workers. This carries with it, however, greater levels of individual accountability and adherence to procedural mandates. This results in a paradox, identified by Rose (1999) in which the professional autonomy of social work allows for its existence as being able to work with difficult and unstable situations while at the same time attracting an increase in the use of monitoring, accountability and discipline which serve to undermine professional autonomy. Inevitably this is then replayed in the interactions between social workers and service users as a form of self-protection on the part of the professional. The difficulty of engaging across the professional boundary is already erected by status. The social distancing effect of professional status has been subject to observation and scrutiny for some time. Being seen to be self-interested, protectionist and elitist is a recognized hazard of professionalism at the same time as being defining characteristics of the same (Mills 1951).

This tension has been defined in terms of a choice between professionalization and proletarianization (Hugman 1991), the latter being an invitation to social workers to organize themselves primarily as workers with a consequent closer association with those they work for and a focus on developing common interests with them while pursuing employment matters through trade union action. This 'radical' perspective on professionalism continues to be promoted outside of mainstream academia and practice (Searing 2011) and has its roots in a direct challenge to the notion of the social worker/user relationship being portrayed as one of superior and subordinate (Davey 1977). Presenting professionalism and proletarianism as dichotomous is however contentious itself. It is possible to take elements of both to enhance the effectiveness of the social worker in their relationship with service users. Extensive knowledge, adherence to a clearly stated set of values, a strong commitment to social justice, discipline, conscientiousness and hard work are professional qualities which can be deployed to good effect in collaborative efforts with service users. This is akin to the 'New Professionalism' as referred to and summarized by Thompson (2006) in which being a professional is less about self-protection and exclusive status and more about deploying elements of professionalism to increase the effectiveness of collaboration with service users to their benefit. An awareness of one's position as an employee does not have to be forfeited in this context. On the contrary, it is more likely to reinforce an orientation towards challenging organizational practices where appropriate. Some authors have argued for precedence to be given to 'values', derived from the worker's motivation to care for and support, in redefining what professionalism is in relation to social work (Healy and Meagher 2004). If social workers are successful in securing such a reconstruction of professionalism within their organizations then a dimension of practice characterized by the development of collaboration beyond organizational boundaries could be established. This has the potential for social workers and service users together to re-assert the creation and validity of new interpretations and knowledge which challenge the received wisdom supporting the superiority of the expert. A contra-indication to this process is the existing splintering of social work in service delivery settings. For successful collaboration to reach outside of the organization professionals need opportunities for collective activity within and across the organization and profession. Much in the way practice with service users is undertaken on an individual/familial basis then so do social workers often operate as individuals with their own caseloads and responsibilities, accountable through linear line management arrangements.

Obstacles to crossing the professional boundary are given greater force by embedding the professional identity with the organizational identity. It could be argued that these should be closely associated in any event but both already struggle with the paradox of public service in the predicament of the drive towards retrenchment of the state and continual downward pressure on public spending. The propensity for the autonomous professional to create and agitate against such constraints is increasingly restricted when service users are likely to perceive the possibility of allegiance and alliances with those on the frontline delivering services being dissipated through the actions of service providers in managing financial cutbacks. At another level the process involved in the appointment of managers often involves either the internal promotion of a professional or the importation of external personnel who may or may not be versed in the particularities of the profession in which they are now actively involved. In all these cases the status and position of the manager are external constructs connected to dominant political and economic drivers. In turn the power and influence of the manager derived from status and position, in this context, are less likely to be intrinsically tied to the professional identity or values of social work. It might in fact be considered a hindrance if they were. One state social worker has presented a view not uncommon in social work circles that 'many of the senior managers have no feel for social work anymore. They are managers, professional managers who have little feeling for the clients' (in Jones 2001: 559). A management approach, for example, is often distinguished by an appeal to working with the reality of how things are in the wider world rather than how things should be. It follows from this that power and influence within organizations, which develops from the collaborative efforts of professional and service user peer groups, will have a greater propensity to reflect the motivations traditionally associated with the intention to enter a caring profession or being a recipient of services.

Several decades ago local authority social workers embarked on a national strike in pursuit of a national pay re-grading claim. This resulted in social workers in several UK cities being out on strike for a number of months. In the city where I worked at the time there were approximately 300 social workers and for the first time professionals from across the city were in contact with each other through meetings and picketing and other strike activities. There was considerable discussion around professional issues inspired by these new found collectives. A major spin-off was the establishment of city-wide 'interest groups' formed around professional practice matters such as child care and mental health. These groups became firmly established post-strike and an embedded feature of the professional structure within the local authority social services department. Within a short space of time discussion and option papers were being produced with suggestions for developments in service delivery, policy and practice. This example highlights the potential for collective approaches to gain credence, influence and power within organizations where individuals create pathways to cut across traditional boundaries of structure and work practices within workplaces. The obvious weakness was the lack of inclusion of service users and others in the process.

A more recent example is detailed by Goodman and Trowler (2011) who led significant changes to the organization and practices in Hackney Council's Children's Services. Their 'reclaiming social work' model, based on systems thinking aimed, among other things, to generate a new organizational culture and structure. The existing bureaucratic, hierarchical structure had reduced social work practice for many to form filling and what Goodman described as conveyor belt social work (Rix 2011). The new model is characterized by acknowledging and encouraging the professional social workers' intellectual skills and creativity and enabling them to work together in a collective 'unit' to deliver a service working with children and families with delegated responsibility for decisions and the delineation of administrative tasks to the coordinator of the unit. This didn't necessarily release staff from adopting approaches driven by managerial imperatives such as 'efficiency' but the change has been positively evaluated by Cross, Hubbard and Munro (2010).

For several decades, however, the elements of accountability within organizations have been mediated through the management who are in turn influenced and directed by wider political determinants which focus on efficiency derived from economic imperatives. Under such direction there is an advantage to the system if management is detached from direct contact with the point of service delivery. This modern phenomenon is more commonly referred to as 'managerialism'. Blok (2012: 180) refers to Brandsen's (1998: 5) definition of managerialism as

> a form of management ... focused on economically defined efficiency and effectiveness and outcome-directed control ... combined with ample power for managers to shift standards. This structure enables the manager to limit the powers of other professionals and to centralize control, and authority within the organization.

In this context the professional social worker functions with limited autonomy as an agent, under direction, in the market place of welfare. For its part the government sets the parameters within which the core activity of assessment of individual behaviours and needs takes place (Gilbert and Powell 2010). This might be interpreted as a perfectly legitimate arrangement within a democratic society were it not for the fact that the parameters set in a political and economic environment dominated by neo-liberal thinking serve to maintain a status quo of increasing social division not least in terms of the distribution of economic and power resources. In a different political and economic context, as Gilbert and Powell (2010: 130) point out, 'The social work profession should support and maintain structural conditions for improving self-regulating abilities of people in the framework of a democratic functioning society with a high standard of quality of life for all.'

'Quality of life' for the service user and the professional alike is a statement about how one evaluates the experience of living in the circumstances in which one finds oneself. If people find themselves divorced from those things which give them a sense of fulfillment and meaning and unable to control or have power over their given circumstances then they can be said to have a low standard of quality of life. The reverse applies. Having a high standard of quality of life means being connected to those things which are fulfilling and meaningful to us. Power and control in our lives becomes extremely important to us. For the professional social worker, processes of de-professionalization, restricted professional autonomy, distancing from service users, bureaucratic requirements and managerialism reduce the quality of the experience of being a social worker. For the service user lack of resources, low pay, unemployment, poor housing, poor access and lack of influence over the social, political and economic processes impacting on them all determine their standard of quality of life. These are the two sides of an equation which militates against a productive and creative relationship between service user and professional and between service users and organizations.

To resolve such an impasse Ferguson and Lavalette (2004) suggest that we first have to understand and apply Marx's concept of alienation. Adopting this perspective it is argued that the processes I have referred to above result in increasing distancing of the individual from control over the sources and nature of their work, from control over the outcomes of their work, from their natural tendency to be creatively productive and from any inclination towards collaborative and collective activity which contradicts the essentially individualistic and competitive forces of the dominant system. Jones's (2001) presentation of the views of state social workers uncovers the impact of 'alienation' on the morale and motivation of social workers. He describes how less contact and direct work with service users, more paperwork, more managerial direction and an emphasis on performance defined externally have resulted in high levels of dissatisfaction and a separation of professional expectation from the reality of the work experience. This is summed up in the words of a worker in talking to a student on placement: 'They [managers] wanted to change the way we do things, relocate and offer a less intensive service. I thought that was a terrible idea, but who am I? It's the corporate bosses who make the decision not the likes of us on the ground who know what happens every day'. We are directed to consider the 'wider canvas' of neo-liberal politics in a western capitalist context to start to understand the manner in which control in the hands of those with power translates into the undermining of the public sector and service in favour of the privatized domain irrespective of which particular political party comprises the government.

Power and service users

Jones's (2001) analysis is reiterated by Ferguson and Lavalette (2004) with the claim that outing the true source of political and economic power in society exposes the real powerlessness of the many. This should not be read as a total denial of the 'power is everywhere' school of thought expressed by post-modern theorists and thinkers. It is undoubtedly the case that power operates every day at many different levels and between millions of individuals and groups. The problem is that adopting a post-modern view should not obscure the validity of exploring power at a structural level, which has often been the case. These are two processes which run in parallel and are interconnected.

For the vast majority of social service users the lack of control arising from their relative position in society is magnified many times over when it is accompanied by the circumstances in which they live, that being in a state of poverty. The distance that service users feel from the ability to control what happens to them can lead to a deep sense of helplessness and in some cases despair. Ferguson and Lavalette (2004: 305) consider the plight of young men who present as anti-social, aggressive 'no-hopers' and conclude that,

> Excluded from a commodified society and culture, denied access to the world of work – or facing the prospect of occasional, casual 'poor work' – divided from and suspicious of others who are portrayed as competitors or a 'threat', increasingly controlled by policing and welfare agencies – these are the social, structural processes of alienation that shape these young men's lives.

The implication here is that seeking to empower such young men through individualistic programmes of intervention may have some impact on some of their interpersonal behaviour but in failing to address the social/structural elements, the overarching conditions creating the situation remain unchanged and the problems will persist either through recidivism on the part of the individual or by re-emerging in the behaviour of others. It is not unreasonable to suggest that in seeking to exercise power individuals may seek out opportunities in areas which circumvent the major forces that dispossess them of power, and these might lead to anti-social and criminal behaviour. Put another way, if individuals cannot achieve through mainstream social avenues then they may attempt to achieve through other channels presented to them in their immediate environments.

The difficulty for social work in attempting to extend its scope of intervention through redirecting its analysis and assessment of situations is exemplified in Saleebey's (2011: 185) espousal of a belief in the power in people delivered with some fervour in defence of 'strengths based' approaches to social work. He states, 'Liberation exerts tremendous pressure on the repressive inclinations of institutions and individuals. Collectively, liberation unleashes human energy and spirit, critical thinking, the questioning of authority, challenges to the conventional wisdom, and new ways of being and doing.' While this connects well with the concept of alienation and its contraindication he continues by focusing almost entirely on a change process involving the psychological reframing of individuals, families and communities. This has the positive consequence of highlighting the need to work with people in collaboration but the objective omits change efforts aimed directly at the source of power and wealth imbalances so firmly embedded in our political and economic architecture. The experience of stress at work offers an organizational analogy. Workplaces are awash with policies and advice on how to deal with stress at work. It does not take any onerous investigation to realize that the entire focus of these is on providing counselling and life coaching advice to individuals who are suffering from the affliction of stress. The possibility that working conditions, managerial structures and approaches, expectations, scarcity of resources and workload may be significant contributory factors is scarcely mentioned.

It is important to accurately ascertain the location and nature of the pathology in order to determine the nature of the problem and devise effective responses. It is insufficient to turn the focus exclusively on the individual or group who are but one aspect of the problem and at the same time the manifestation of the other aspects which lay outside them as individuals. The powerful in society are protected from challenge by pathologizing the individuals who are the victims of decisions made by these same power brokers. In January 2012 unemployment among 16–24-year-old people in Britain exceeded the figure of 1 million for the first time since records began with 22 per cent of this group being out of work and never having obtained a secure job in their adult lives. The consequences of this in terms of social problems will be various and substantial and individual young people will make choices which will either improve or worsen their situation but they will all be decisions, for better or worse, which make sense in the situation in which they find themselves. The pathology here does not lie at their doorstep and any social work response must reflect an approach to problem definition which does not render empowerment meaning only the 'correction' of individuals in the face of such stark social injustice.

In situations where the service user is seen as in need of care as opposed to control there continue to be subtle and not so subtle mechanisms which undermine their ability to determine what happens to them. It might be acknowledged that service users are experts in the field of their own experiences and needs but as one social work student observed, 'Service user involvement can at times seem tokenistic in nature and ultimately does not seem to be the defining aspect of policy development and implementation' (student dissertation, 2010). Wherever service user participation is limited or absent then the existing imbalances in power between them and practitioners and organizations is exacerbated. This becomes most evident in conditions of economic recession and cuts in public expenditure when service users have little or no say in what services are reduced or withdrawn, even though these impact directly on them. Social workers find their power directed towards managing rationalization while attempting to challenge and resist against the impact on service users. They operate as both powerful and powerless in different directions at the same time, a state all too often characteristic of the professional role. This increases the tension between working at the level of the individual and seeking to effect structural change. Healy (2000), among others, has highlighted the tendency in social work to opt for individual practice-based solutions rather than shifting priorities to addressing structural forces and the discourses which reinforce the social reality confronting service users.

Decisions on where to allocate spending invariably centre on issues of risk and need deficit rather than strengths, support and human rights. Users may turn to the facility to complain under the Children Act 1989 and the National Health Service and Community Care Act 1990 which also made it a legislative duty to consult with service users on the planning and delivery of services (Dalrymple and Burke 2006). Power relationships play a significant part in the effectiveness of such measures. Complaints procedures provide for individuals to seek redress for actions of maladministration and poor practice but this is limited to proving that the service provider either failed to meet its obligations under law or failed to follow due process and policy in reaching its decisions. If you are not happy with the service you receive or have had requests for provision declined, the facility to complain, while opening some channels of communication, proves largely oppositional in practice and highly individualistic. Some difficulties may be resolved for individual service users but complaints procedures do not, as a rule, afford a power base to users, collectively or individually, to positively participate in shaping service provision or service levels. In this way the service user is responded to as a consumer rather than empowered as a citizen. It is for the individual consumer to complain if the product is unsatisfactory rather than the provider promoting opportunities for democratic participation in the core decision-making processes.

The shortcomings in making democratic participation a reality for many are illustrated by the comments of staff involved in working with older people as related to a social work student on a masters programme. This presented a largely pessimistic picture of participation even where structures were in place. One member of staff observed:

> Service users have a limited amount of involvement. I have experience of service users groups and committees, but I honestly couldn't name one piece of practice that I know changed as a result. If a person's wishes appear to be impossible due to the level of service in place then it won't happen.

Another lamented that,

> Most services are still woefully short of service user involvement except during inspections. In these instances 'users' are not seen as knowledgeable and experienced i.e. as experts, so the basis for meaningful involvement is not recognized and acted upon. User involvement should be a day to day activity and not a one off or seldom used activity.

Including users in organizational matters is only one aspect of user involvement and tending to be locally focused can work to incorporate and dissipate potential challenges to the underlying design, structure and resourcing of services on a wider level. Blok (2012: 91) draws us to a more radical and wide reaching approach to involvement reminding us that

> Notably, much of the progress in our civilization has occurred because of people who united and fought to liberate themselves and their children and grandchildren from oppression, poverty, discrimination and degradation. As long as individuals continue to come together and form united fronts, social change and progress will continue.

User organizations recognize that there is a wider struggle entailed in bringing about meaningful change in power relationships in society. One example is provided by the People First Lambeth Group which supports people with learning difficulties to speak up for themselves. A member of the group in 'An Urgent Letter to the Government' (People First Lambeth 2010: 10) prompted by impending reductions in public funding, states, 'The cuts could leave us with nothing. We could have no choice in our lives and no power. If the government are cutting all our jobs we have no say in the matter.

They should have talked to us first [about] what we want in our lives because this is ridiculous.'

As Beresford (2011) has said greater awareness or insight on the part of service users as a result of their experiences has led them, in many instances, to reject the idea of social workers empowering them and to place the emphasis on empowering themselves. In the fields of mental health, disability, abuse (whether of children or women) and offending user movements have arisen, often as a consequence of the services offered being experienced as oppressive (Payne 2006). This is then combined with a realization that survivors have a capacity to resist particularly when they join together collectively. This implies that social work is effectively redundant in the process of service user empowerment. Taking the statement from the letter above, however, we can see how it represents the commitment and ability of people to make their own voices heard but at the same time embodies the limitation of the voices in the face of the power of government to ignore the protestations. In addition there are many groups who struggle to have a voice and those that do may work less effectively in isolation than in alliance. Asylum seekers, homeless people, dementia sufferers, and those in poverty are a few of the disparate and diverse groups that have little voice but are in need of support, services and resources. These people can improve their chances of being heard through alliances with professional groups such as social work, and social work could make a difference through its own organizational, professional and political networks in collaboration with service users and their organizations. It is in this arena that the core political identity of social work is discovered and its value-based social objectives fought for. Re-defining the interpersonal relationship with users, working to expose organizational constraints and seeking to ally with service users at different levels, social workers can 'be engaged in a constant search for the means by which these relationships can be transformed in the interests of those who are losing out' (Smith 2008b: 212).

Key points

1   Power is a social concept which we evidence through its impact on people and their attempts to acquire and apply it in everyday activity and is inextricably linked to the value base and ethical position which social workers adopt in their practice.

2   Social workers should aim to attempt to achieve a professional relationship in which there is a two-way process with clear dialogue and in which power factors undermining this are minimized.

3   Social workers have to be keenly aware that their actions can either help people gain more control or undermine their efforts and further disempower them.

4   If we accept that power is relational then in all circumstances of social work intervention there is the potential to change or modify these relations.

5   Most people's sense of powerlessness is derived from dispossession and marginalization as products of the economic and political systems directing their lives.

6   The fact that people protest or challenge demonstrates that it does not follow that social forces 'determine' the responses of either the service user or the professional; rather people might recognize these forces as 'obstacles' against which they can react.

7   The discrediting of professional practitioner knowledge is part of a wider process of de-professionalization through which the control of professionals becomes more manifest.

8   Being a professional is less about self-protection and exclusive status and more about deploying elements of professionalism to increase the effectiveness of collaboration with service users to their benefit.

9   There is potential for collective approaches to gain credence, influence and power within organizations where individuals create pathways to cut across traditional boundaries of structure and work practices within workplaces.

10   Pervasive relational power and structural power are two entities which run in parallel and are interconnected.

11   The powerful in society are protected from challenge by pathologizing the individuals who are the victims of decisions made by these same power brokers.

12   Obtaining power can be facilitated through alliances of professional groups and service users using the organizational, professional and political networks available to them.

Questions for discussion

1   How can social work address the relations of power which undermine and oppress many women in the personal, familial, organisational social and political dimensions?

2   How can social workers positively redefine the power relations with service users in times of severe financial constraints in the public sector?

3   In what ways can social workers respond to processes of de-professionalization and managerialism to effect meaningful participation of service users in service design, planning and delivery?

5 Poverty, disadvantage and social work

'the poor have disappeared from the culture at large, from its political rhetoric and intellectual endeavours as well as from its daily entertainment.'

(Ehrenreich 2010: 117)

Politics, policy and poverty

I am writing at a time of economic recession in the major western economies when the word poverty is re-entering the lexicon of the debate around relative wealth, income and access to resources. For some time now the phrases 'social inclusion' and 'social exclusion' have dominated the discourse in this area enabling politicians and others to divert the discussion away from questions of redistribution of wealth and concentrate on matters of education and work as the keys to resolving the resilient presence of significant inequality in our society. This was the hallmark of the 'New Labour' government's approach in the UK between 1997 and 2010 during which the route out of poverty was from 'welfare to work'. This has continued under the current Conservative-led coalition government. In this way the role and responsibility of government, business and policy makers becomes that of providers of opportunities for people to grasp and if they do not take advantage of these then the cause of any resulting disadvantage can be justly laid at the door of those claiming deprivation. In this way the aetiology of social problems, including poverty, can be explained as the results of choices that people make and political leaders can claim moral neutrality in promoting this perspective (Orton 2009).

This, however, only accounts for one aspect of the issue, i.e. that people make choices that affect their prospects and relative position in society. This idea of 'agency' as purposive human action (Deacon 2004) has to be placed in an understanding of 'agency within structure' (Orton 2009). Orton continues by stating that the 'either-or' and 'both-and' approaches to agency and structure do not wholly capture the experience of those on low income and in debt. It is 'agency within structure' that matters and the decisions people make which affect their life chances and financial and wealth predicament are critically influenced by their experience of their structural location and the social forces conspiring to maintain them in their current state. Orton found that low income as a structural factor, in particular, played a significant role.

The omission of structural causes and the word poverty from the mainstream debate on inequality can be balanced by the observation of Mantle and Backwith (2010) that the critical perspective in social work is traditionally associated with a focus on poverty as a structural problem. The latter, they suggest, has nonetheless been undermined by the dominance of the neo-liberalist ideology of the times with an emphasis on individualistic approaches. Poverty certainly impacts on the lives of individuals and is 'associated with just about every social ill one can think of and with which social workers grapple' (Mantle and Backwith 2010: 3). It is the poor that social workers work with (irrespective of which perspective they take on its nature, cause and solution), with the majority of service users being in poverty and nine out of ten in receipt of state benefits (Becker 1997). Trevithick (2012) highlights the fact that social workers work almost exclusively in areas of urban deprivation and neglect and with the most disadvantaged sectors of the population. A realization of this is a first step to devising practice which fits this fact and reflects the social work aspiration of achieving social justice.

The extent of the problem is illustrated by the level of segregation between children in poverty and those not. In the London Borough of Tower Hamlets using official measures 52 per cent of children live in poverty while only 5 per cent experience the same condition in Hart in Hampshire (End Child Poverty 2012). It should be noted that the official measure of poverty is an income of below 60 per cent of the national median household income. One is said to be in severe poverty where income falls below 50 per cent of this median.

The Chief Executive of the Child Poverty Action Group, Alison Garnham, is quoted as saying, 'The Child Poverty Map paints a stark picture of a socially segregated Britain where the life chances of millions of children are damaged by inequality' (Elks 2012: 11). The same report presents an overall situation in which one in five children in the country is living in poverty. Garnham, in evaluating current government policy claims that,

> Ministers seem to be in denial that, under current policies, their legacy threatens to be the worst poverty record of any government for a generation ... They risk damaging childhoods and children's life chances, as well as our national economic wellbeing from wasted potential and social costs spiralling. It would be a catastrophic failure in public policy and political leadership.
>
> (Coughlan 2011)

Brewer et al. (2011) in the Institute for Fiscal Studies commentary on poverty and inequality, predict that child poverty will have risen from 17 per cent in 2010 to 23 per cent in 2020 against a government target of 5 per cent by 2020 set in 2010. They also indicate that 6.5m adults will be in poverty by 2013 (2.5 million with children and 4 million without) while the bulk of the population will experience the most severe drop in median income in 35 years.

Modern increases in poverty were most evident in the years of the Conservative Government of Margaret Thatcher from 1979 to 1990 when numbers in poverty rose from 5 million to 14 million during a period of radical change towards the welfare state and the role of government (Alcock 2006). A comprehensive portfolio of policies was adopted aimed at reducing state intervention through low taxation, reducing public spending, supporting the free market, widespread privatization of publicly owned industries and utilities, undermining trade union influence, promoting individual responsibility and reducing state welfare. These policies were aimed at increasing growth in the economy which would ease poverty through a general uplifting of living standards to be derived from the 'trickle down' effect. Although the already wealthy saw significant increases in their wealth this would translate into an overall increase in wealth in the economy and would have a knock-on impact to the benefit of all through increased incomes and charitable giving.

The legacy of these years remains a core feature of the social and economic policies of successive governments up to the present. Jones and Novak (1999) illustrate what to them is a clear and predictable failure of the 'trickle down' effect to distribute wealth more widely and evenly. The response to this failure by New Labour was to introduce a number of schemes targeting the harsher consequences of free market operations to promote the emergence of 'soft', 'compassionate' or 'caring' capitalism through what was termed 'The Third Way'. Although there was a reduction in official levels of child poverty by some 600,000 between 1997 and 2010, overall levels of poverty and the experience of its effects have shown little change in the intervening years and have been exacerbated by the financial 'crash' of 2008/09 in the western world. Many leading politicians, as a consequence, are responding positively to the call for the development of 'caring capitalism' to alleviate the damage of unemployment, low wages and increased benefit restrictions to the many millions of people affected. Concurrently there is a defence of what is considered an essential continuation of the key elements of reducing the national budget deficit through existing coalition government policies of low taxation, reduced public spending and reductions to benefit payments and pensions.

Some commentators argue that it is sometimes difficult to get full sight of the 'caring' image. For example, under current government proposals the terminally ill and those with disabilities on state benefits who sit within the Work Related Activity Group (WRAG) are to be pressurized to work without pay for unspecified periods of time with no guarantee of paid employment or face having their benefits cut (Malik 2012). In the same article Neil Bateman, from the National Association of Welfare Rights Advisers, complains that the proposals offer 'completely inadequate legal and medical safeguards [and] compulsory unpaid work may worsen some people's health . . . people should get the rate for the job, instead of being part of a growing, publicly funded, unpaid workforce which, apart from being immoral, actually destroys paid jobs' (Malik 2012: 2). Other bodies including Disability Rights UK and MIND have expressed similar objections or concerns. Policies to significantly increase the minimum wage or to develop interventions to ensure a living wage across the employment sectors are assessed as potentially damaging to the economy. The preferred strategy for making work pay as a way out of poverty is to reduce welfare benefits, increase the rigidity of eligibility testing for people with disabilities, cap pension increases to the lower index of price increases, the CPI (Consumer Price Index), and to cap housing benefit allowances to tenants. Irvin (2008) has advised that growing inequality has the effect of reproducing ideas and politics which make inequality seem natural and people more callous towards its consequences.

It remains to be seen what impact these policies will have but there is a danger that they may result in greater numbers of homeless people, people being forced to move from their communities and increases in child and older person poverty and poverty in the wider society. The voice of the poor is marked by its absence from the policy debate. This is of direct concern to social work in being asked to work with the victims of recession, support them and at the same time ration the decreasing resources available. As one social work student contemplated in her analysis of poverty and social work, 'People who are vulnerable and need society's help the most are ignored due to the ignorance of society' (anon 2011).

Absolute or relative: recognizing poverty

Social workers will be one of the first professional groups to be directly confronted by the consequences of poverty. It has a devastating effect where 'poor men and women very often express a sense of hopelessness, powerlessness, humiliation and marginalisation' (Narayan et al. 2000: 32), and has a particular salience for certain groups. As Mantle and Backwith (2010) warn, the lives of young people and ethnic minorities are blighted by unemployment and low pay while recession brings further misery to those areas already disadvantaged. Although the 'New Labour' government from 1997 on set targets to reduce child poverty in direct response to the unparalleled increase in the wealth discrepancy between rich and poor witnessed during the previous 18 years, these were not achieved and we are once again witnessing a widening gap between the two. The effects of poverty are not confined to those defined as poor by the drawing of official arbitrary lines. By focusing on the effects in psychological and physical terms one can justifiably argue that poverty stretches well beyond current thresholds and is an experience of those with incomes above the 60 per cent of mean income cut off point. Many millions on low pay with poor working conditions could justifiable lay claim to falling into the 'poor' category, struggling to survive financially with all the consequences of personal and familial pressures which take their toll on living standards, quality of life, personal relationships and self-esteem. Older people are a specific example of a group where many do not fall below the 'poverty line' but the majority are found to 'cluster' around it so have similar experiences of deprivation and are three to four times more likely to find themselves in poverty in the UK than in other European countries (Price 2006). In the case of children, 58 per cent of those classed as in poverty live in a household where one or two adults are in paid employment and this figure is increasing (Child Poverty Action Group 2011).

From a social work perspective it is far more useful to define poverty in terms of people's experiences than to struggle with the academic debate on the relative merits of the differing concepts of 'absolute' and 'relative' poverty. This debate, which tends to centre on seeking a scientific definition of poverty, often proves interesting yet fruitless for practitioners and frequently results in a consensus around the use of both in a multi-dimensional approach. Although it may be important to apply a benchmark of income, wealth and living standards for the development of social welfare policy and social security measures it is far more appropriate in working with people to capture the reality of the consequences of inequality through a multi-dimensional approach. As Alcock (2006: 80) says, 'multiple indicators capture the different dimensions of different aspects of poverty, and are likely to have different implications for the focus of anti-poverty policy'. To move beyond the absolute/relative debate still leaves the observer with the position that it is not possible to appreciate what poverty is unless it is juxtaposed or compared to wealth. For Jones and Novak (1999: 18) in a modern capitalist setting the two 'are bound up in a dynamic relationship in which one produces the other'. It is the same for the relationship between poverty and wealth as it is for that between the powerless and the powerful: the one cannot exist without the other and one cannot be described without reference to the other.

In turning one's attention globally it is possible to demonstrate a severe inequality of position when comparing the poor in the UK to the plight of the poor in some countries with little or no developed welfare systems, infrastructure, public services or wealth distribution policies. The former may well appear to be in a preferable condition. This does not, however, allow for the conclusion that addressing wealth and income differences domestically is inappropriate or should be of less priority. Many of the poorer populations of nations globally are subject to the same economic and social processes as the poor locally due to the mechanisms of the prevailing economic system, albeit to varying degrees. It is these processes that need to be confronted and addressed rather than attention being diverted to making decisions on who is more or less deserving. Social work is culturally and legally specific to the country in which it is practised so is best equipped to deal with the local effects of these processes even if 'such nationally framed practice is unable to cope with social and economic trends that are global in dimension' (Paylor and Washington 2000: 110). A further error would be committed by allowing any such comparisons to result in underestimating the extent of the deleterious effects of poverty, as experienced in the UK, on even the most basic aspects of human need and aspiration in everyday life.

It is reasonable to contend that poverty or the threat of it is not the preserve of an officially designated minority but affects large sections of the population, including many in paid employment who struggle to acquire the necessities of life for themselves and their families in an attempt to avoid the stigma of being identified as poor or threatened by poverty. The fragility of sustaining a standard of living which allows for relative comfort in work, leisure and pleasure is nowhere more starkly exposed than in the sight of professionals including teachers, doctors and others queuing to receive hand-outs from soup kitchen stalls set up in the streets of Athens in 2012. It is understandable that many people will try to distance themselves from those identified as the poor or as members of an underclass, and then passively or actively acquiesce in the prejudiced attacks made on the poor and benefit claimants by governments and media until such time as circumstance contrives to render these same people in similar positions.

The concept of the 'underclass' arose in the 1970s as a sociological categorization of those who fell outside of existing definitions of class distinction or relations (Spicker 2007). Groups who were experiencing long-term unemployment, poverty and deprivation and thereby appeared to be permanently outside of mainstream society most readily fell ripe for this categorization. It is true to say that a number of writers and politicians have previously referred to this concept from a position of sympathy for those so categorized (Alcock 2006), but it is also evident that the term has increasingly been and is now mostly used to draw attention to undesirable character traits and deficient attitudes and motivation among many poor people who for all our best efforts will remain 'outside' due to their own peculiar and even mysterious ways. This 'blame the victim' perspective clearly plays into the hands of the dominant discourse on the poor as explored and explained by Jones and Novak (1999).

Living in poverty

What are the impact and experience of living in poverty? The effects of poverty span areas of housing, employment, relationships, physical and mental health, education, longevity and mortality. Finding yourself in one of the categories most often linked to social work intervention such as having a disability, being old, being an asylum seeker, homeless, or a child in need makes you more vulnerable to the unwanted consequences of relative poverty. Where poverty is prevalent communities witness increased levels of behavioural problems particularly in boys. Poor and inadequate accommodation/housing together with a lack of local resources for youth activities and personal and family support heighten the incidence of these problems (Hooper et al. 2007). This report on living with poverty by Hooper and colleagues for the Frank Buttle Trust showed that children who had only reached the age of 5 were worried and stressed while in some instances they were very concerned about the situation confronting their families and for some this made them unwilling to look to their parents for support. They experienced a more violent living environment in their communities and in school. Feelings of being unsafe, held by adults and children, were joined by problems of bullying, abuse, domestic violence, drug misuse, relationship breakdown, and mental health problems. Some 250,000 5-year-old children are unable to dress properly, and lack levels of concentration and the ability to speak and recognize words when set against educational standard targets (Ramesh 2012).

Of particular relevance is the likely link between poverty and increased referral to child protection services and legal interventions to place children in care (Vornanen et al. 2011). In the UK in January 2012 the monthly number of Public Law Care Requests rose to 903 (CAFCASS 2012). This is the highest figure since the Children and Family Court Advisory and Support Service was formed in 2001. This increase is being related to greater sensitivity to the effect on child welfare of drug misuse and domestic violence in families (BBC 2012). These are, in turn, exacerbated by poverty so it is cogent to note that since the beginning of the current financial crisis in September 2008 the number of these Care Requests has risen from 483 per month to its current level. Although being in care may offer some protection from immediate threats to a child's welfare there is considerable evidence that it does little to improve one's life chances and attainments. The Department for Education and Skills (2006), with its aim of improving the lives of children and young people in care, refers to what it described as some shocking statistics on education. These include an educational achievement level of only

11 per cent of children in care attaining '5 good GCSEs in 2005 compared with 56% of all children, and similar performance gaps existing at all ages both before and after Key Stage 4' (p. 2). This report entitled *Care Matters* also directs us to the devastating nature of the long-term outcomes of children in care: 'They are over-represented in a range of vulnerable groups including those not in education, employment or training post-16, teenage parents, young offenders, drug users and prisoners' (p. 2). In this context poverty can result in your participation in a system that, at best, will often provide you with a parallel experience of deprivation and underachievement in preparation for adulthood.

Despite this, many of the children in the Hooper study aged 5–11 were positive about their own futures and had ambition and aspirations for good jobs. They were not resigned to a life of poverty but had to struggle with a poverty of life in the here and now as a form of abuse through societal neglect. Over time such pressures and growing social awareness can reshape the individual's view of future prospects in a less than positive way. Although families valued the support offered by services that were reliable, trustworthy and accessible, these were 'helping people through' rather than changing circumstances or opportunities. The availability of this quality of service is curtailed in areas of deprivation further undermining people's coping mechanisms. As Goodman and Gregg (2010) have pointed out, the often preferred approach of governments in trying to improve aspirations in the parents of poor children to improve the latter's opportunities and life chances may have some validity but this appears to be limited to treating a symptom of poverty and will have little impact on educational (*or other*) achievement unless the socio-economic causes of poverty are tackled and its effects ameliorated. Where accessible quality services are already limited there is a potential for a disproportionate impact when further reductions in public spending and fiscal reforms are made. In assessing the effect of cuts in services to young people being implemented by the present coalition government in the UK, Michael Marmot is quoted as warning that 'Cutting services has a selective impact the lower down you go in the social hierarchy. We see increases in child poverty and are moving from direct to indirect forms of taxation, which are regressive. I am really concerned about these things and their impact [on inequalities] (Ramesh 2012: 10).

The findings of Hooper et al. (2007) are supported by Martin and Hart (2011) who summarize the findings of a consultation organized by the Office of the Children's Commissioner. This study surveyed the views and experiences of young people aged between 10 and 20 and living in some of the most deprived areas in England. Many lacked basic equipment for their education such as pens and books and it was wrongly assumed that they had ready access to computers. This lack undermined their potential for academic achievement and also affected their social connectivity. They had to do without possessions and activities which they saw others enjoying such as certain clothes, meals out, cinema and holidays. These young people felt shame and suffered from bullying, being singled out at school on non-uniform days and being unable to afford school activities and trips which encouraged them to withdraw from school. Their parents were forced to work long hours and for seven days a week trying to do the best for their children who observed that this, with a lack of resources, put stress on their families, produced high levels of conflict within the home and sometimes led to family breakdown. It also meant that young people did not have the means to move on to independent living and faced marked difficulty in obtaining employment or felt a strong responsibility to get a job for the family income rather than continue in education. One young person is quoted as saying, 'Young people are the hardest hit. They are going to end up stuck in a cycle of poverty because they can't get the education ... they can't get the jobs ... they can't escape from it' (Martin and Hart 2011: 11). This gives a sense of young people's keen awareness of the social context of their predicament and the difficulties in defending against the structural relationship of being in poverty when compared to others. Individual agency is represented by the various attempts by themselves and their families to survive their plight let alone improve their situation and, on the other hand, where people turn in on themselves in a negative way in the absence of any means of escape. In these instances we can see how the success of personal agency is directly contingent on the power of the structural forces at play and does not in itself appear to be a significant factor in the aetiology of the circumstance of poverty. This is best stated by the young people themselves who Martin and Hart (2011: 12) concluded did 'not want to be a lost generation, especially as being so would be no fault of their own'.

Many young people's hardships do, however, fall below the radar of public knowledge and scrutiny. Locally in Liverpool this year, 2012, I have spoken with the manager of a local service for young people. Demand for their services from young people aged 10–25 years has risen dramatically in the past year. They see these young people and hear their stories on a daily basis. Many of the young people using these services have come through the care system and on moving to independent living find themselves placed in poor standard hostel accommodation with little direct follow-up from social workers because of pressure of caseloads. Some of the young people claim that the government's 'cap' on housing benefit entitlement means they can no longer pay the rent due. They further say that on occasion private landlords have carried out an eviction with no notice, removing their belongings and changing the locks on the property they were renting. They are left homeless and jobless and in the case of young women this can leave them vulnerable to exploitation by older males. With new employment programmes offering unpaid work placements and more rigid application of benefit rules many claim to have found themselves having their Jobseeker's Allowance stopped, either because they have missed a single appointment with their adviser at the 'job centre' or have failed to sustain attendance at an eight week, 30 hour per week unpaid work placement which they have been directed to undertake. These are the daily experiences related by a number of young people in one of the UK's major cities which will undoudtedly be replicated across the country. Life will already have been a considerable struggle for many of these young people from their early years on. The experience of what they perceive as punishment for failing to meet the demands of mainstream society will simply add further injury to their fragile resources of resilience which have been tested throughout their lives as they wander the streets between visits to the local voluntary service which they value.

Where you live and the quality of your accommodation is directly linked to health outcomes. Housing inequality and health inequality are inextricably tied as pointed out by Shelter (2009). This Shelter report paints a picture of poor people living in poorly insulated, fuel inefficient and inadequately repaired houses. It outlines the serious implications this has for residents' health particularly children who suffer dispropor- tionately from a range of conditions such as meningitis, asthma, other respiratory problems, skin conditions, anxiety and stress while their adult carers show increased instances of depression and mental health difficulties undermining their capacity to care and nurture. Approaching 50 per cent of all childhood accidents are linked to the physical environment at home. These accommodations are largely found in the private rented sector and social housing where many less well-off people are forced to live and rising fuel prices do much to make matters worse as often these dwellings necessitate the use of more fuel by virtue of their condition. In other instances people are living in a temporary residence, which has been shown to contribute to mental health difficul- ties (Mitchell et al. 2004). Shelter (2009) highlights that those sleeping rough for long periods and those in hostels experience increased rates of TB and hepatitis compared to the general population. They have more respiratory problems, skin diseases, injuries following violence, infections, digestive and dietary problems and rheumatism or arthritis. Almost half of all young offenders will have been homeless at some point.

Mortality rates among the poor, particularly for those with mental health difficul- ties, have been found to be nearly five times higher than for the matching age group in the general population (Marmot 2010). Although life expectancy for the general population is rising year on year the gap between that for the poor and the well-off is widening and can stretch to a 15-year difference in some areas (Ramesh 2012). End Child Poverty (2012) offers further insights into the damaging effects of poverty. If born in a deprived area you can expect to live seven years less than in a relatively wealthy area and you are likely to have a lower birth weight which markedly increases your chance of dying as an infant or having a chronic disease in later life. You will most likely show lower attainment cognitively and educationally while, up to the age of 14 years, you are five times more likely to die in an accident than your well-off counterpart in a professional family. Up to 8 per cent of parents cannot afford more than one pair of shoes for each of their children and 12 per cent of lone parents do not have the finances to buy presents for their children or arrange celebrations on their birthdays or other special occasions.

Before you make it to your mid/late teen years you are 15 times more likely to die in a fire in your own house. Roberts (1995) explains that the risk of fire is linked to the type of housing you live in with those in the poorest social housing or living in temporary accommodation being at highest risk. Being a lone parent also puts you in this category. Although some 86 per cent of households now have smoke alarms (DfCLG 2011) those on low incomes or in rented accommodation tend not to have smoke alarms installed which leaves them without the single most effective protec- tion from death resulting from fire. Roberts promotes the use of structural therapeutics through professionals advocating for better quality social housing, increased benefits for loan parents and legal responsibilities being placed on landlords for fire safety measures on their properties. Such an approach requires a structural understanding of the problems of poverty. Any consideration of the detail of the experience of living in poverty should immediately alert the social worker to the import of including this as a vital dimension in the construction of a meaningful professional assessment. Of course, the way in which social workers and other professionals respond to the consequences of poverty will depend on their orientation towards the nature and cause(s) of this phenomenon, which in turn should be derived from a detailed knowledge of the experience of living in poverty and not solely from an evaluation of dominant discourses on the issue.

Causes and solutions: agency and structure

On first reading the work of Oscar Lewis (1961) I was absorbed by the stories of the members of the Sanchez family in Mexico and the manner in which they saw how life was, their behavioural responses to it and how people in their community interacted, constructing a particular way of life in the face of severe poverty and lack of opportunity. Lewis undertook ethnographic studies in Mexico and Puerto Rico and developed the concept of the 'Culture of Poverty' which was popularized through its adoption as the basis for government policy in several western countries from the 1960s onwards. Such is the power of the idea that it has permeated much of the ideological thinking sympathetic to claims that much of the problem of poverty arises from the ways of life of the individuals, families and communities that experience it. This is particularly popular among governments of a right wing political persuasion but is evident, as we have seen, across the political spectrum and is to be repeatedly observed in popular culture through the media and other forums of dialogue.

Lewis (1961) concluded that there were certain discernible features of a culture of poverty. Present-time orientation referred to a marked tendency not to look to the future so aspiration, ambition, planning and motivation were all sacrificed for a focus on what was happening day to day. This was accompanied by an inability to defer gratification with individuals acquiring what they could when the opportunity arose and indulging in immediate pleasures where and when they could be obtained rather than giving consideration to saving or gathering resources for more secure and long-lasting improvements in one's lot. The meaning placed on their position and role in the wider society led to responses of resignation and fatalism, a feeling that they just had to get on with how things were and that their futures were set in a way that meant they would be unable to change things. This culminated in a sense of not being a part of society but marginalized and separated from it.

All these features can be linked back to a range of observations and commentary previously made in this chapter. The main contention about the causes of poverty derived from this theoretical construct is that the poor behave in similar ways and pass these behaviours on through generations so that they become part of the people's culture. As it applies to individual human thought and behaviour this thinking lends itself to universal application across the industrialized west and countries developing under the capitalist umbrella where success is seen to come from individual self-improvement and effort. This trans-generational transmission of poverty thesis has become a political system of belief underpinning most modern approaches to combating poverty.

The pathologizing of individuals who are deficient in the human qualities required to function adequately in society provides a (popular) rationale for targeted policies such as Sure Start, reforms to raise educational achievement in poorer areas, unpaid work schemes (compulsory internships), youth employment schemes and benefit penalties. These are all aimed at intervening at key points in people's lives to divert them towards a new way of thinking and behaving which enables them to lift themselves out of poverty. It is intended that this will have a cumulative effect of progressively ending poverty because people will no longer behave in a poverty promulgating way and will instead grasp the opportunities afforded them by society in a context of equality of opportunity. The 'culture' of large sections of society will be changed permanently and the causes of poverty with it. The retrenchment of the welfare state acts as a necessary parallel incentive for this to happen.

Looking back at the Sanchez family, as representative of poor people, it is possible to reframe culture as adaptation if we apply agency within structure to what we observe. In any situation humans may adapt to the circumstances that surround and engulf them. This does not mean that they engage with the experience positively or positively propagate it or promote it. At an individual level people may adopt ways of surviving or flourishing, in their terms, while not being contented or happy with their predicament. Some individuals will fight to better themselves and some will join to create collectives to challenge wider societal structures and processes seeking the fairer distribution of wealth and resources. Ruth Lister (2004) acknowledges these adaptations in calling for us to respect personal agency and poor people's ways of negotiating their lives. To reduce the cause and solution to poverty to resistant culture is to oversimplify the issue and allows the redistribution of wealth to be taken off the agenda of possible options in the fight to end poverty.

Imagine a room filled with hundreds of people shoulder to shoulder with only one entrance door and one exit door. Beyond the exit door is a world of relative plenty while inside resources are very limited. Everyone is shuffling around attempting to gain access to the exit door but only a small number of people are allowed through every year. Some will devise strategies to manoeuvre near to the exit and remain in the vicinity awaiting the chance of escape. Others will lack the wit or guile or physical capacity to do so and could well find themselves shuffling for the rest of their lives so will either find ways of adapting or will deteriorate through ill health, mentally and/or physically. In the meantime more people are arriving through the entrance door because they have lost their job or grown older and lost income or find themselves as lone parents on low income with children to provide for or are young and have been unable to obtain employment. This situation is problematic. If you approach the solution from an individualistic, cultural view of the situation you are likely to introduce into the room the means by which people can increase their motivation, intelligence or skills. But no matter how much you put in the total number inside the room will remain relatively stable, first because of a 'bottle-neck' at the exit, second because those exiting are being replaced by those entering and third because those in power on the outside own and manage the resources available and determine the number of opportunities allocated. If, however, we examine the structural picture presented we might consider increasing the number of exit doors or a planned removal of the walls, breaking the barriers between those inside and the possessors of power and wealth on the outside. Overseeing the distribution of available resources more evenly may follow.

This societal analogy demonstrates the interactional operation of the two major causal forces of poverty of agency and structure and implies a proportional relationship between the two weighted in favour of the structural impact. All attempts at explaining the causes of poverty involve a debate around the relative weight which should be afforded to each (Alcock 2006). This question is of central importance to social work and the balance of the respective roles of agency and structure in this is an essential element of accurate and effective professional assessment and intervention. As Soydan (1999: 43) states, 'The nature of the causes of social problems is one of the fundamental questions in social work. The nature of these problems may be seen as a dichotomy (i.e. "society generates social problems" or "the individual generates social problems") or as active interplay between these mechanisms.'

Western social policy, in modern times, has been largely based on ideas of individual agency as moulded by community culture as being at the root of problems of deprivation and marginalization and these resonate with western governments' attempts to attack poverty and its consequences going back some 50 years. This political rhetoric is still with us suggesting that this approach has had little success in achieving its core aims and has reaped few rewards in terms of changing the nature or levels of poverty in the medium to long term. President Lyndon B. Johnson in proposing to the US Congress the Economic Opportunity Act of 1964 declared the 'War on Poverty' in the USA intending to employ policies of intervention in early childhood through targeted education programmes, work experience schemes for the unemployed and character building camps for unemployed youth. He was not looking beyond the door of opportunity in declaring that his policy would 'provide a lever with which we can begin to open the door to our prosperity for those who have been kept outside' (US GPO 1965).

Although some reduction in overall poverty was witnessed in the decade following the War on Poverty (which came to an end in the late 1960s), and a number of its policies have continued at various times in different shapes and forms, there has been no evidence of any lasting impact on levels of poverty in the USA with most recent official indicators showing a poverty rate of 15.1 per cent or over 46 million people. This is the highest number since poverty data was initiated in 1959 (DeNavas-Walt et al. 2011). When set alongside the UK statistics and experience of continued welfare reform aimed at individual behavioural change as cited earlier, the validity of the 'Culture of Poverty' as a general theory of the cause of poverty can be seriously questioned. Nonetheless it persists in the thinking and actions of policy makers, and business owners and the protestations of politicians.

Spicker (2007) sets out what he sees as six main classes of explanation for people becoming poor. These are individual pathology, familial factors, sub-cultural explanations, distribution of limited resources, structural causes and institutional agency failings. These can, however, be grouped under the two main contenders, which I have so far identified, as agency and structure. As we have seen the personal 'agency'-based explanations for the existence of poverty include ideas about pathological deficits of character or behaviour in individuals, the influence of family upbringing and the behavioural shaping of the cultural context of neighbourhood, community or ethnicity. The alternative major perspective is proffered by the structural school of thought which includes the classical theories of Marx, Weber and Wright Mills. This turns our attention to the way in which social and economic relations are organized in society and divisions along lines of class, ethnicity, gender, disability and age define the boundaries across which inequality can be seen and measured. In many instances older people, the unemployed, children and people with physical or learning disabilities are seen to offer little to the productive processes of modern capitalism and therefore are more likely to be dependent on social security thereby receiving the least monetary reward and appearing disproportionately among the poorest in society. Poverty here becomes a symptom of a specific policy aimed at controlling as well as providing basic support to the disadvantaged (Novak 1984).

The American sociologist Herbert Gans has long argued against the 'agency' approach to poverty as espoused in 'culture of poverty' ideas claiming that 'the prime obstacles to the elimination of poverty lie in an economic system that is dedicated to the maintenance and increase of wealth among the already affluent' (Gans 1971a: 156). Elsewhere he demonstrates, with some wit, how poverty is highly functional when viewed from the perspective of the higher economic orders in society (Gans 1971b). He lists some 13 aspects of social function which the poor fulfil. These include, doing the low paid 'dirty work' that others will not but which is essential to daily social activity and maintenance; providing domestic service to make it easier for the middle classes to pursue their aspirations of career advancement and material possession; creating employment for those who deliver services to the poor (including social workers); keeping the aristocracy busy and giving them a reason for being through charitable patronage; and stabilizing the political system by not participating in it to any marked extent, leaving it to those with a vested interest in maintaining the status quo. In return, Gans claims, the poor pay the heaviest cost for economic growth when they have laboured to construct modern cities only to be displaced from their neighbourhoods and communities to make way for those who can afford to occupy the fruits of others' work. The industrialization of agriculture shifts people from working on the land to a life of urban poverty while for many of the young poor, recruitment to the armed forces to fight wars across the globe, risking injury and death, is a readily available and readily promoted opportunity.

The state and the market

Structural thinking shifts the focus from individual causation by the poor to those with power and wealth in society. It is argued that 'the existence and extent of poverty in advanced industrial societies is the result of a choice made by political authorities, economic elites and middle-class electorates' (Myers 2010: 128). The motivations of certain groups must nonetheless be derived from some systemic imperative. In other words, we have to ask the question, 'What is it that brings these groups together to form an alliance, whose actions create inequality?' One answer might be found in exploring the mechanism of free-market capitalism on the premise that it is most often economic forces and decisions which determine political direction and social policy.

If the objectives of the free-market in a globalized context are to facilitate production and exchange of goods, the free movement of capital and the accumulation of wealth through profit then certain requirements are set before nation states which strongly influence the political, social and economic circumstances of their populations. The requirements of the free-market include:

- low taxation and reduced public spending as incentives to work and to invest;
- depressed wages for the general workforce to improve worker motivation and maximize profit margins;
- unemployment as a means of holding wages down and as a motivator to seek or stay in employment;
- increased competition between workers for jobs and higher wages, undermining collective action and threats to the system;
- minimal state intervention in industrial and financial regulation for the healthy operation of the market;
- reductions in state welfare and social security to promote individual responsibility and reduce public expenditure, thereby helping to keep taxation low;
- increased privatization of industry and services (including social and health) to maximize opportunities for profit and private wealth creation;
- unemployment as a by-product of economic fluctuations;
- residual welfare to ensure the reproduction of a healthy, reliable labour force;
- managed collective power among workers to facilitate positive industrial relations while minimizing the threat of revolutionary action.

The claim is that in combination these provide the dynamic which enables wealth to be created through economic growth which benefits all. The evidence of persistent inequality and poverty in nations acts as a persuasive counter to this claim and a structural analysis would lead to the contention that it is these requirements in operation which lead to inequality and poverty.

In the current (2012) crisis within the eurozone the primacy given to maintaining the free-market dynamic stands as witness to its own impact in creating extremes of poverty and potentially undermining national democracy. In 2012, political leaders in Greece and Italy have been replaced by unelected premiers who the European Union Commission will monitor and expect to implement policies in accord with the requirements listed above. We are seeing the results of this in what are termed 'austerity' measures to reduce national deficits, which are resulting in destitution for many thousands of people in Greece, for example. The system preserves itself at the cost of many citizens' livelihoods and futures. The economic elite are able to protect themselves and preserve their status by moving their wealth to where it is less vulnerable and invest in other forms of wealth such as property and land which can be acquired more cheaply in times of economic hardship for the many.

The influence of the state is tempered, and this is accepted even in the view of some on left of mainstream politics. Jones and Novak (1999) cite New Labour's position on the free-market in the 1990s reflecting that the party had no argument with those who reap rich rewards from the system and will ensure the market is fair to those who don't. They refer to the Labour Manifesto of 1992 as stating, 'Modern government has a strategic role, not to replace the market but to ensure that markets work properly' (Jones and Novak 1999: 181–2). Does this indicate an underestimation of the strength of the free-market system or an overestimation of the strength of the state? George and Howards (1991: 91) resolve this in claiming, 'In brief, poverty is the result of the capitalist system; it can be reduced somewhat by government policies but it cannot be abolished within capitalism.' It certainly denotes the potential for concluding that the market does not necessarily act in the interests of the majority of the people and in the process renders many of them in a state of relative poverty. In some instances, particularly those of economic slow-down or depression, the state will actively participate in the process of creating poverty as in the case of Greece and other western democracies where 'austerity' measures are implemented. According to Wachtel (1972: 193) poverty is indeed 'A logical consequence of the proper functioning of the capitalist institutions of class, labour markets and the state'.

The role of social work

The International Association of Schools of Social Work (IASSW 2001) makes the rather grand claim that social work 'In solidarity with those who are disadvantaged . . . strives to alleviate poverty and to liberate vulnerable and oppressed people in order to promote social inclusion'. Although a useful signpost to locating social work in the social, political and economic relationships contributing to poverty, it is not safe to assume that this is the manner in which social work has or does conduct itself in its workings with poor people. The influence of dominant neo-liberal ideology and its attendant individualistic ideas on the causes of poverty will not have failed to enter the thinking of the profession or the content of its training courses. The institutional, state sponsored nature of both renders them more likely to incorporate mainstream thinking and practice. Mantle and Backwith (2010) warn us to expect this while pointing to the critical/radical tradition in social work which, taking a structural stance, has long focused on poverty and deprivation as central concerns for social work.

It is true to say that social work has had a long and complex relationship with the poor and poverty and that the majority of service users experience poverty. Becker (1997) having confirmed that up to nine out of ten service users are benefit claimants, raises the interesting contradiction between the thinking and practice of social work. The results of his research indicate that social workers are very positive in their attitude towards the poor and see their predicament as a result of injustice and structural forces yet when it comes to their practice they adopt largely individualizing methods of work which are aimed at helping the service user adapt to their circumstances. While seemingly paradoxical it does not appear so unreasonable when set against the organizational, political and legal constraints placed on ways of working available to social workers. In recent calls from the co-chair of the National College of Social Work, Corrine May-Chahal, for social workers to be more involved in eradicating child poverty the emphasis was not on campaigning for structural change but for a widening of involvement to incorporate work in early years intervention and education to enable greater social mobility through improving individual ability (Pemberton 2010b). This resonates closely with the nature of the long-standing relationship that social work has had with poor people and their communities.

Since the days of the Charity Organisation Society (COS) social work service has been separated out from the giving of financial support save in specific preventive circumstances and has been orientated towards seeing the problem of poverty as being a problem of the poor themselves. Jones (1998: 120) reminds us of the message from leading COS members that 'social work's task must avoid any materialistic strategy of financial relief and be focused on improving the character of the poor to ensure that they adopted as their own, values of thrift, sobriety, self-reliance and independence'. This is both a personal and political statement. You resolve poverty by saving people from themselves while, at the same time, ensure social stability and progress by bringing the poor into the mainstream in terms of their values and behaviour. It is interesting to note the intellectual consistency between thought and action here as contrasted with more recent tension between thought and action as described by Becker (1997) above. The attitude of professionals may have changed with time but their practice is still largely in keeping with historical precedent.

Social work has struggled with this ambiguity and paradox for decades chiefly as a result of its context of delivery as discussed in earlier chapters. This includes being a state controlled service under the influence of neo-liberal politics, the related organizational processes of managerialism and regulation and the major theoretical perspectives informing its methods of practice. The strength and political convenience of the 'pathology of the poor' way of thinking has ensured its continued incorporation in social policy developments which set the framework and detail of social work practice. In the post-war period up to the late 1960s psychoanalytic thinking dominated social work methods with its heavy emphasis on diagnosis of adult types displaying pathology of the mind as expressed through dysfunctional behaviour and relationships.

The emergence of sociological explanations of social problems and behaviour led to little more than amendments to mainstream approaches with the introduction of psycho-social approaches which retained a heavy emphasis on the 'psycho' side of assessment and intervention. Behavioural and person-centred humanistic methods, although challenging psychodynamic ideas, have continued the tradition of focusing on changing people rather than social structures and relations. Notable exceptions have been incorporated including anti-oppressive and service user led approaches which have attempted with varying levels of success to articulate and popularize particular alternative methods in working with dispossessed and deprived service users albeit by often focusing on disparate elements along lines of race, gender, sexuality and disability.

The one common tie that remains is that whichever group you belong to the one thing that you have in common as users of social services is that you are most likely to be poor. These recent approaches to social work practice represent current manifestations of the radical/critical arm to social work which has endured in different forms since the 1960s, promoting welfare rights work, community activism, service user participation and campaigning with and on behalf of the poor. In addressing the systemic nature of poverty social work is more likely to become part of the solution to poverty rather than part of the problem and avoid 'itself becoming an increasingly uncritical tool of the UK government's social authoritarianism' (Gilligan 2007). Social work will need to analyse and be transparent about its relationship to poverty as the two remain closely linked despite the ironic observation of Beresford and Croft (2004: 58) that 'the creation of the welfare state and the ending of the poor law more than half a century ago, were meant to signal the end of this link'.

Key points

1   Reference to poverty has been replaced by the use of terms social exclusion and inclusion over a long period enabling governments to divert discussion away from questions of wealth distribution.
2   The decisions poor people make are critically influenced by their experience of their structural location and the social forces conspiring to maintain them in their current state.
3   There is a very serious problem of inequality in the UK both in terms of the divide between the wealthy and the poor and the distribution of this divide geographically.
4   Social workers are one of the first professional groups to be directly confronted by the consequences of poverty.
5   The effects of poverty are not confined to those defined as poor by official arbitrary lines.
6   It is far more useful to define poverty in terms of people's experiences than to struggle with the academic debate on the relative merits of the differing concepts of 'absolute' and 'relative' poverty.
7   The effects of poverty span areas of housing, employment, relationships, physical and mental health, education, longevity and mortality.
8   The causes of poverty can be seen as either lying in the personality deficits and ways of living of the poor or in the structural relations and processes in society.
9   The economic forces and decisions of free-market capitalism determine political direction and social policy.
10   Social work has had a long and complex relationship with the poor and poverty.
11   The attitude of professionals may have changed with time but their practice is still largely in keeping with historical precedent.
12   In addressing the systemic nature of poverty, social work is more likely to become part of the solution to poverty rather than part of the problem.

Questions for discussion

1   Social work is located in a set of relationships with the state and its agents, the economic system, service delivery organizations and the poor. Detail the ways in which these relationships shape social work practice with the poor.
2   How far are poor people responsible for their own predicament?
3   How might you start to develop ideas from anti-oppressive thinking into concrete methods of practice?

6 Psychology, sociology and social work

Much of the content of the discussion in previous chapters includes representations of different ways of thinking about the phenomena covered derived from perspectives in social sciences, in particular psychology and sociology. Identifying a 'world view', recognizing and developing a guiding set of practice values, seeking to use or dissipate power and accounting for the nature and causes of poverty which blights the lives of so many service users place demands on the professional to possess a knowledge and understanding of many processes of a personal, social and political nature. In order to explain, account for and defend their practice social workers need to be able to demonstrate this knowledge and understanding in their thinking, discussions and writing about their practice at several levels. This will include the specifics of case assessment, planning and intervention or in more general considerations of social work delivery and the relations between the different groups and interests involved.

Any consideration of agency and structure in exploring social work practice sits within a framework where psychology and sociology act as areas of knowledge underpinning approaches to working with people. In large part psychology as applied to social work has provided a basis for focusing on the thoughts, feelings and behaviours of individuals and families with a view to assessing how it is that people react to and behave in different ways in their environments. To this extent psychology should offer some insights into the 'agency' side of the equation. Theories drawn from sociology have diverted attention towards aspects of the environment outside of the individual which have direct or indirect influences on the way people behave. This brings us closer to an awareness of the structural elements and processes of society which affect everyone on a day-to-day basis.

As we have seen there is a continuing debate as to the relative impact of each of agency and structure on people's functioning and ability to cope. Is the demonstration of public anger by an individual in poverty a symptom of a psychological 'fixation' caused by unresolved 'oral' stage dissatisfaction or a normal reaction to the frustration of attempts to live like others without the resources to do so? In terms of where to look for the cause and resolution of problems, the answer to such questions has far reaching implications for how professionals think about and work with people who are referred to them. The previous chapter led us to the conclusion that the historical context and current political location of social work have resulted in a practice which emphasizes a psychological agency focus when thinking about people and their problems despite a clear acknowledgement of the structural influences which trap them. I have, for example, clear memories of writing reports for court which would contain just one short opening paragraph outlining the social/environmental circumstances of the individual involved, and how this results in the disproportionate incidence of certain types of behaviour which was a symptom of a wider social malaise unrelated to the individual perpetrator. This would be followed by a lengthy account of the individual's personality, upbringing, interpersonal and familial relationships and schooling exploring the nature of the personal 'pathology' that had led to this person appearing before the court. A counter proposition was brought to my attention recently in the form of a report to court in which criminal behaviour was reframed as normal and rational in the face of certain social forces. The case presented was that society had so clearly failed to meet the perpetrator's basic needs of food, shelter and safety that it was inappropriate to expect this person to show concern and respect for the basic needs of others.

In Chapter 2 several of the 'grand' theoretical premises were discussed, including functionalism and Marxism, with the aim of assisting in the search for a 'world view' so it is perhaps helpful at this point to consult, critique and reflect on some of the major psychological perspectives which underpin much of direct social work practice. This together with further consideration of macro- and micro-sociological approaches which are increasingly playing a part in practice developments might help to inform further thinking on the nature and balance of ideas in problem analysis and practice in social work.

The biological

For the physiological psychologist human biology offers most of the answers to why people behave, think and feel in the way they do. I recall from my own undergraduate days the enthusiasm with which one or two of my teachers looked forward to the day when all would be explained by genetics, chemicals and electrical impulses. They saw the task as working to identify the components within these categories which taken together will produce behaviours across the full spectrum of human activity. This is seen as a highly scientific approach through which human behaviour can be 'reduced' to clearly definable, testable and evidenced causes. Bell (2002) describes this 'reductionism' as seeking understanding of complex matters by reducing them to simpler parts resulting in a single explanation for what is being observed.

The influence of biological thinking in social work practice is not to be ignored and it is constructed as one arm of the medical/social model debate which draws on the juxtaposition of nature and nurture (Barker and Davidson 1997). In mental health work the dominance of the medical model persists with interventions being primarily designed around drug-based solutions and developments in diagnosis resting largely on research into genetics and the electro-chemistry of the brain.

Work with young people is also subject to ideas framed within biological thinking (Timimi 2005a; Timimi and Taylor 2004). The use of drugs to 'control' ADHD and the manipulation of diet to manage behaviour are but two examples. More recently we have witnessed social work participation in asylum seeker age assessments using biological examination and data (Pemberton 2010a). In such circumstances 'free will', choice and cognitive processes are seen as non-contributory and therefore irrelevant. The ability to simplify the complex interaction between the physical human entity and the myriad social systems with which they interact will be an attractive enterprise to some but should invariably present the social work practitioner with testing moral dilemmas.

From a political viewpoint finding 'answers' to social problems is facilitated by the more straightforward solutions offered by biological interventions. The more extreme examples afforded by history act as reminders of how science, when divorced from considerations of human rights and cognition, can lead to the principles of professional practice being seriously and dangerously compromised. Johnson and Moorhead (2011) in their exploration of the role of social work in Nazi Germany demonstrate how it is possible, given conditions of ethical uncertainty, for social work to comply with the requirements of governments in ways which contradict its stated aims and principles. Johnson and Moorhead (2011: 7) paraphrase Ife (1997) in saying, 'Contemporary social work today grapples with the issue of ensuring global social work practices are ethical and value human worth, while faced with the demands of government policies that in many cases have the potential to control and oppress the disadvantaged.'

Vigilance in recognizing when social workers are asked to act in ways which might contravene values of human worth, dignity and potential is called for particularly in situations where the findings of biology are appropriated by those institutions charged with addressing social problems. This is not a statement of opposition to biological research or the use of advances in drug treatment per se. It is not the technology itself that we need to ward against but how and by who it is used and the ease with which we believe in the 'truth' of science. Barney and Dalton (2006) suggest that social work, being always located in a political context, requires full awareness of what its practice aims are, and whether these are consistent with what it does in responding to individual and social problems. Professionals in Nazi Germany believed in the science of social eugenics and acted in ways consistent with this belief. Johnson and Moorhead (2011: 8) advise that social work practice should be premised on 'a mandate based on human rights discourse' and go on to say, 'When in a position of asking people to change or conform, what is it exactly we want them to be? More importantly, is it consistent with our values and human rights ideals, and considered in the context of potential structural oppression?'

The psychodynamic

Sigmund Freud is perhaps one of, if not the, most famous psychologist who never trained as a psychologist. He developed the theory of psychoanalysis from which psychodynamic ideas have developed over the past 100-plus years. It is not surprising that this perspective has such pervasive influence given that it provides a universal theory of personality and a therapy the basis of which is largely untestable conjecture but fascinating in its apparent insight and believability. Its key contentions include the importance of the unconscious in human behaviour (Ingleby 2006). The unconscious is the seat of internal dynamics which surface in ways of thinking, feeling and behaving which can only be explained by inferences drawn from reference back to itself (Milton et al. 2011).

These dynamics are expressed in the relationships between three mental structures: the id, the super-ego and the ego (Malim and Birch 1998). The first is the receptacle of the instinctual sexual and aggressive drives with which we are born. These are the driving force of life and continually seek satisfying. The second is the internalized conscience that directs us to respond in a moral way in direct contradiction to the id and is the incorporation of moral codes imputed from our parents and other significant adults in early life. The third is that part of us which presents to the outside world, manages the conflict between the id and the super-ego and attempts to negotiate with the external human and physical environment in a non-self-destructive way (Chung and Hyland 2012). It is the strength of the ego by which we measure our ability to cope with life and this, in turn, is 'determined' in our early years through the stages of psycho-sexual development during which the internal dynamics evolve and are played out and the ego's negotiations with the real world take form. This not only presents a rather 'pessimistic' view of the potential for change but also places a considerable burden on the ego and thereafter it has to employ 'defence mechanisms' to help it avoid overbearing distress and anxiety.

In psychodynamic thinking the mechanisms for and roots of behaviour are clearly located in the individual and if anything goes wrong then the cause and solution can be found in the internal workings of the individual as represented by a weak ego incapable of functioning adequately. Other theories which have a high profile within social work practice developed from or were deeply influenced by psychoanalysis such as 'attachment theory' (Howe et al. 1999) and 'life-long development' theories such as Erikson's eight stages. One of the attractions to social work of this orientation is the emphasis on the personal professional relationship as the route to compensating for early trauma or poor parenting/caring experiences.

One does not have to practise psychoanalysis to appreciate other messages of the theory which can be incorporated into social work methods, i.e. that childhood experiences can be a determinant of adult troubles and that internal conflicts are replicated in our behaviour and relationships through 'transference' or the use of unconscious defence mechanisms (Howe 1992). Without accounting for wider social/cultural arrangements this can present some difficulty. Much of child care assessment in social work focuses on parenting and this often results in working with mothers only, which continues to carry the danger of reinforcing ideas of 'mother (female) blaming' even if this is not made explicit. This may not only reinforce existing social divisions along lines of gender but more generally bolsters certain political reactions seeking to place responsibility for social problems on those that are experiencing them.

Psychodynamic theories in all cases of people problems primarily direct the professional to the weakness or deficiency in the ego/personality for assessment and resolution of their difficulties. This reductionist approach involving unconscious dynamics also affords power to the skilled helper to interpret the behaviour of the service user as the latter, by definition, does not have access to the source of their concerns. In other words they lack insight. However well intentioned, there is little room here for empowerment in the process of intervention and any protest by the recipient can be further interpreted as symptomatic of a dysfunctional ego.

To possess awareness of the elements of relationship that psychodynamic thinking has highlighted might be of use, but not as a means of applying the theoretical specifics of psychodynamics to our work but as a means to maximizing our skills of empathy. Tavris and Wade (1995: 456) remind us that research into the use of the psychotherapeutic method in all its forms suggests that 'The factor that best predicts beneficial outcomes is not the therapist's intellectual philosophy but the patient's perception of his or her empathy.' This becomes particularly salient in working in an anti-racist way which rejects the Eurocentric nature of psychodynamic therapies and their consequent failure to incorporate the significance of the experience and identity of black people, which requires an understanding of the operation of racism in society (Robinson 2009).

Learning theory and behaviourism

Learning theory offers a much more optimistic view of the potential for people to change than psychoanalytic ideas. The latter is rejected as it is considered fruitless to speculate on that which you cannot observe or demonstrate the existence of. With behaviourism you work only on what you can see, hear and measure so you will always know whether your interventions are successful or not. There is a fundamental claim that all behaviour is learnt and therefore can be unlearnt. Our personalities are representations of our learning histories and are no more than an accumulation of behaviours into patterns. If someone is troubled or not functioning satisfactorily then psychodynamics tells us that we have to address the underlying, internal conflicts and feelings that provoke the unwanted behaviour. Learning theory tells us that by attending to the behaviour and changing it people's feelings and emotions will improve and they will function more effectively (Tavris and Wade 1995).

There are several processes through which behaviour can be learnt and unlearnt and these fall within two main forms of conditioning (learning), classical and operant. Ivan Pavlov is most closely attached to the former and Burrhus Frederick Skinner to the latter. Classical (or respondent) conditioning relates to learning by association whereby any natural reflex behaviour can be elicited by a stimulus considered to be neutral (Hayes 2002). For example, being cuddled and stroked will invariably make a baby smile and make contented noises. If another stimulus, such as particular toy was present each time the baby was stroked and cuddled then eventually the presentation of the toy alone would be sufficient to produce the smiling and noises in the baby.

For Skinner (1991), a major proponent of operant (or instrumental) conditioning, all behaviour is controlled and it is the consequences of behaviour which control it. The consequences of behaviour can be either reinforcing or punishing, the former increasing the likelihood of a behaviour being repeated and the latter reducing the chance of a behaviour being repeated. Skinner believed strongly in the use of positive reinforcement as the means to creating a happy society (Chung and Hyland 2012). Positive reinforcement occurs when something pleasant or rewarding follows a behaviour and negative reinforcement results from something unpleasant being removed

Consequence	Positive	Negative
Presented	Positive reinforcement	Punishment
Withdrawn	Punishment	Negative reinforcement

Figure 6.1
Source: Adapted from Kazdin (1975).

following a behaviour. In each case the behaviour is likely to be repeated. Punishment makes repetition of behaviour less likely by following it with an unpleasant event. It can be either physical or mental/emotional or both. The processes of learning in operant conditioning can be presented as in Figure 6.1.

More effective learning appears to take place with positive reinforcement as punishment is problematic in several ways. The punisher often acts in anger without thought and the recipient may well respond with fear or anxiety creating further difficulties in the relationship. Punishment is often presented with some delay after the event undermining the ability of the recipient to link the two. The unwanted behaviour may continue when the punisher is not there to witness it. It is wrong to assume that what we think is punishment will not in itself be positively reinforcing. A child being emotionally neglected might find that the only attention it receives is when the parent/carer punishes it for unwanted behaviour. As attention in the form of punishment is the consequence then the unwanted behaviour is likely to be repeated.

Behavioural work has been very popular as a method in social work for several decades and has been promoted as a valid, verifiable evidence-based approach (Sheldon 1982). Change takes place by manipulating the circumstances of behaviour so that altering what happens before (antecedent) which cues behaviour or what happens after (consequence) has a direct impact on what behaviour takes place. If a parent is advised to play with a child rather than ignore it then the child is less likely to misbehave to gain attention and its good behaviour is reinforced by the parent's participation in a pleasant activity. This approach does go some way to moving the focus from the individual to considering the interactions between people but takes little notice of the more distant antecedents of social conditions which might be adding considerable pressure on the individuals involved. Does controlling behaviour in these circumstances, although aimed at helping, have the potential to take on the characteristics of social policing? Given what has already been stated about hegemony and the internalization of oppression can we be confident that the prescription for changes in behaviour is written by the service user(s) or is it the product of powerful vested interests seeking to maintain social stability and cohesion in an unequal, unjust society? This is a dilemma which professionals have to confront in balancing the personal, social and political in their practice.

A criticism often made, although hotly contested by its supporters, is that behaviourism is deemed to be mechanistic, over-simplifying and neglecting more human cognitive features of conscious intention and subjective purpose (Taylor 1967; Malim and Birch 1998). As a result power differentials between the professional and the service user might be exacerbated in using methods derived from its principles. At one level this appears to be addressed in combining the ideas of behaviourism with those of cognitive psychology with the emergence and increasing dominance of Cognitive Behavioural Therapy as the method of choice in many areas of intervention into social problems (Sheldon 1995). By rehearsing behaviour and its consequences the service user is facilitated in constructing alternative ways of thinking about situations and translating this into future behaviour with associated reinforcements forthcoming from their living environment (Healy 2012). A young offender might be helped to more fully realize the consequences of his actions for others and come to realize the positive outcome for himself of behaving in a different way. Questions of cause and resolution of problems are seen as located in the thoughts of the individual. To reduce the matter to one of faulty thinking facilitates the design of a manageable intervention whose success is the responsibility of the service user. It is obvious where the finger of blame can be pointed in the event of failure by those who are disposed to benefit from publicizing such conclusions.

Humanistic psychology

A psychology which rejected both the 'mechanistic' features of behaviourism and the 'deterministic pessimism' of psychoanalysis and assumes the inherent goodness of human kind has found great favour with the people oriented professions such as social work. The names of Carl Rogers and Abraham Maslow are now in the minds and on the lips of every social work student and practitioner. Their work is based on the premise that given the right environment everybody has both the capacity and the intrinsic motivation to change and develop their behaviour for themselves (Rogers 2004). This is allied to the ideas of phenomenology which is concerned with the mind, and thereby subjective experience is given primacy in trying to understand the human condition.

Rogers proposed that given the central importance of the subjective then the concept of 'Self' becomes particularly salient (Malim and Birch 1998). Although his and other humanists' thinking presents a very positive view of human motivation it also acknowledges that the environment gets in the way and can cause problems for people specifically in the form of poor relationships with significant others. We may well be motivated to become 'self-actualized' but certain conditions need to pertain to achieve this, one being a healthy portion of 'unconditional positive regard' whereby we are loved for who we are and not for being how we think others want us to be (conditional regard). If our developing years are marked by an unhealthy imbalance between the two with a surfeit of the latter then we are likely to experience high levels of incongruence between whom we think we are and who we would like to be (Chung and Hyland 2012). This extreme discomfort of existence leads to severe difficulties in coping day to day and various levels of mental distress, which themselves result in us relating to people and doing things in a way that confirms our existing problematic view of ourselves.

The concept of self-actualization, which we are all motivated to achieve, was introduced by Maslow (2011) and he placed this at the apex of a hierarchy of needs. 'Deficiency motives' covering physiological, safety, belongingness and esteem needs sit

a daily basis through reading papers, magazines and watching television. The observer has to 'read between the lines' to reveal the 'message'. You might, for example, wish to note the relative importance, content, tone and length of a news item to detect bias for or against a particular person, institution or viewpoint. The cumulative effect across the full range of communication forums should not be underestimated. The media, in turn, is owned and/or influenced by powerful vested interests, including the BBC, so the force of these influences is considerable.

We have already considered some of the consequences of this in earlier chapters in discussing the outcomes of the social processes involved and their impact on the people who are most likely to come into contact with social workers. An interesting 'grass roots' counter to these influences is the growth of democratic communication via the global network of the 'World Wide Web' on the internet. The potential of this medium to be used by and for the benefit of service users in collaboration with social workers has yet to be fully exploited by social work. As a professional body it continues to struggle to prevent the arena of digital communication becoming another dimension of social division consequent to lack of access and control by marginalized groups (Parton 2008; Steyaert and Gould 2011). By reflecting on the influences shaping social work thinking the profession can be more certainly in a position to offer the kind of informed contribution which Habermas thought so important to the achievement of 'communicative competence' discussed earlier in this book (Outhwaite 2009).

An important claim of critical psychology is that psychology is political in nature and psychologists play a political role (Chung and Hyland 2012). This is by virtue of its location in a similar complex of social, political and institutional frameworks to social work. We can extract from this that as psychology and social work are practised in a multi-professional arena then all health and social care activity is political activity. This moves us away from individualist to collectivist thinking and the relevance of a Marxist analysis of the difficulties confronting the oppressed, deprived and marginalized in society. This begins by looking at their relative positions in the economic system which controls the distribution of wealth and resources, then analysing the workings of the various institutions of government, industry and finance which impact on people's lives while operating to preserve the dominant economic system. This way of understanding of human behaviour redirects the professional to incorporating a focus on the institutions of society, including their own employer as targets for change. This facilitates a reframing of their work with individuals to do less 'fixing' (Howe 1987) of the service user and more freeing up to challenge the external sources of their problems.

Power in relationships, at all levels, is highlighted in a critical psychology perspective. Feminist psychology has challenged psychology to address its own inequalities and to expand its study of issues pertinent to women free from the sexism of existing dominant psychological theories and the prominence of males in all areas of research, teaching and organization. In essence feminist psychology calls for the voice of women to be increasingly heard in the subject (Wilkinson 1996). It would be erroneous to characterize feminist thinking as homogeneous in nature but the common ground points to the obvious way in which psychology has acted to prop up sexist ideas about men and women. In general being male has been used as the norm or benchmark for measuring sex differences so that research outcomes have tended to place women in negative categories of deficiency such as, having lower self-esteem, undervaluing their own efforts, being less self-confident, having more difficulty developing a separate sense of self, and being more likely to say they are 'hurt' than to admit they are angry (Burman 1998).

These characterizations have worked their way into the social psyche, supporting and promoting existing stereotypes, and clearly have to be guarded against in our personal and professional lives. In the case of the latter it is worth reminding ourselves that women constitute a significant majority when it comes to caring for children and others in need in both a personal and a professional capacity and are much more likely to come under the scrutiny of the authorities with direct contact from their professional representatives. This gendering of social work intervention as a 'hidden' oppression is in addition to the professional focus of attention on the poor and deprived in our society.

The way in which children and young people and the social problems with which they are associated are viewed in western society is contested by critical ideas. The modern western concept of childhood as a developmental period of becoming an adult leads to paradoxical personal and societal reactions (Morss 2002). This can be seen in British society where, in general terms, attention is drawn to the need for protection and nurturing while at the same time there is a cumulative 'ageist' effect. This results in children and young people being treated as not quite full human beings, to be controlled, not really listened to, punished as part of a learning/maturing process and largely marginalized so that they are treated with suspicion if not supervised by an adult. Reframing childhood as a state of being, of worth in its own right provides a route to achieving the goals of inclusion, having their voice(s) heard and improving understanding of their perspective on relationships, behaviour and society while recognizing that they are vulnerable by virtue of their size and inexperience (Burman 1994). This emphasizes the need for social workers and other professionals to reflect on their own internalization of received wisdom on childhood constructed from the dominant discourses of mainstream psychology.

Issues of anti-social behaviour and ADHD are brought into relief by the critical approach in psychology which contextualizes behaviours which are construed as personal deviance. While the lived experience of many people stands witness to the destructive consequences of some behaviour by individuals and groups the anti-social category has become a broad umbrella for all that is considered an intrusion or disruption to adult activity by younger people. It is those living in poorer areas who are targeted leading to working class youths being criminalized and politicians emphasizing the need for ever increasing social control and behaviour regulation (Waiton 2006). When set in a context of dense, poor quality housing, few resources for youth, the appropriation of space by cars and the communal tendency of adolescents many behaviours can be seen to be problematic by virtue of their location rather than being intrinsically deviant in nature. At a simple level this can be illustrated by stating that the noisy neighbour in a terraced street is no longer a noisy neighbour if set in a living environment where houses are spaced by virtue of wealth and land ownership.

The acts of individuals provide a convenient smokescreen to hide the more enduring social devastation created by poverty and inequality (McMahon 2006). Critical psychologists present a persuasive case for replacing many issues from a personal to a social and cultural context where the increasing intolerance of behavioural diversity can be more readily confronted. Mainstream definitions of social problems are reinterpreted as elements of a strategy to maintain social cohesion to protect the interests of the powerful and wealthy. Timimi (2005a) and Radcliffe and Timimi (2005) relate the manner in which the diagnosis of ADHD has evolved by reference to an ever increasing yet 'authoritative' check-list statement of behaviour criteria with no identifiable biological basis. They point to the many fold increase in diagnosis and prescription in Britain and the USA since the 1980s as evidence for the political and social constructionist nature of the condition. We are left as a society regulating the behaviour of our children, in their thousands, through chemical means.

With the increasing awareness afforded by a critical perspective students can analyse the content of their learning of psychology on social work courses identifying several aspects of the source of theories including the social, political and cultural background of theorists, their sex, the context and sponsorship of research and theorizing, the historical and geographical location of theories and theorists and the aims and intention of research. All these can be used as legitimate areas for questioning. Psychological theory and the practice methods derived from it should never be unquestioningly accepted solely on the basis that they are scientifically objective but should be explored to determine in whose interests they operate and what potential they have for perpetuating inequalities and injustice.

Overarching social narratives

The coverage of the essentials of functionalist and conflict theories in earlier chapters identified some of the difficulties of functionalism in that it assumes that the institutions of society, family, government, the legal system, churches and the economy all work together for the purpose of social well-being and the maintenance of society as a cohesive whole. An analogy with the human body is often made demonstrating how it is maintained by the individual organs working through interconnection for the whole (Cunningham and Cunningham 2008). It also takes for granted some shared value system that individuals sign up to of their own volition.

Assumptions of this kind are ripe for challenge once we explore the origins of the 'consensus' or what Knuttila and Kubik (2000) call 'normative orientations' as a tendency to an agreed way of thinking. They argue that the functionalist line of argument becomes difficult to sustain once its tendency to minimize the impact of inequality, conflict and contradiction in society is exposed. We have just witnessed the levels of inequality resulting from the prevailing economic system. Can such a system be said to be working for the whole of society? Do differentials in power and vested interests play a significant role in the determination of what should be the so-called moral and behavioural consensus? The fragility of such claims of unity and cohesion can be observed in the strength of call from those with political power, in the face of increasing social division, to condemn protestors as 'Trotskyist thugs' or stating 'We are all in this together' proposing that rich and poor alike feel the pain of economic hardship in equal measure. Market capitalism is seen as a given which we just have to cope with in periods when it does not work so well. Any acknowledgement of a core function of the market as a creator of inequality and social division is sacrificed or denied with a determined defence of its merits and the diagnosis of failure being directed at its victims who are seen as lacking in the ability to grasp the opportunities it presents. A case in point is found in the words of the managing director of the International Monetary Fund who referred the solution to the current (2012) financial crisis in Greece back to the Greek people who she claimed had not been paying their taxes and that now it was 'pay-back' time (Elliot and Aitkenhead 2012).

Such calls to cohesion and order around acceptance of current social and economic arrangements resonate with the belief in the self-seeking individualism which Hobbes (2010) and Locke (2010) had located as the essence of a fixed and universal human nature whose needs could only be tamed through socialization into market-based interaction and exchange. There is, however, a considerable literature drawn from anthropology and other disciplines which suggests there is a major difficulty with asserting a single human nature or limiting social relations to market competition (Knuttila and Kubik 2000). Challenging and questioning what appears as a social given or fact should be a permanent item in the informed professional's tool kit.

For the practitioner, conflict theories and Marxism in particular present a different set of problems. The deterministic inevitability of the economic system controlling all other elements of society immediately offers a rather pessimistic view of the potential for change and built on to this are the system and society's changes and adaptations which have occurred since the writings of Marx and have resulted in a much more splintered view of how society is divided up and operates. Ralph Dahrendorf (1959) setting out his thoughts on 'post-capitalism' offers a critique of Marx's thinking on class conflict, claiming that while conflict is still a central feature of social and economic life this is now less about class and more about relations of power and authority.

Suggestions of a less complex class system persisting are undermined by people's own perceptions of relative wealth, power and control and the interactions of powerful groupings in society which variably operate either collectively or in competition, e.g. the state, the church and business (Inglis 2012). The years of 'Thatcherism' and 'New Right' thinking and action which followed the emergence of radical social work approaches in the 1970s saw the growth of managerialism, surveillance and regulation of state social work (Cunningham and Cunningham 2008) which has served to depress alternative 'Marxist'-based practice orientations at a time when the predictive quality of Marxist theory has been all but rejected in academic dialogue. It is nonetheless still possible to analyse these changes from a Marxist perspective and the relevance of economic exploitation, alienation and false consciousness remains in analysing the condition of people in the post-modern world. Dahrendorf (1959: 64) cites the levelling of social life experiences in modern times as indicative of a decomposition of class conflict in classical Marxist terms but does not deny the existence of conflict or inequality:

> In so far as the theory and practice of equality in post-capitalist societies are concerned, it seems certain that they have changed the issues and patterns

of class conflict, and possibly that they have rendered the concept of class inapplicable, but they have not removed all significant inequalities, and they have not, therefore, eliminated the 'causes of social conflict.

If there is conflict across many dimensions and groups in society as pluralist theorists suggest then it is not a competition of equals. When considering all the groups in society competing for resources and influence it is possible to discern a pattern in which a clear division appears between the 'winners' and the 'losers', with the latter constituting the groups that social workers work with. This is not about bad luck or the fair operation of the market. It is about the preservation of divisions in wealth, education, connections and self-protection among the powerful, which is largely outside of the control of the individual. In other words one's relative position in the economic order as determined by one's position in the market is the main determinant of one's ability to access the necessary resources for a satisfactory quality and standard of living.

This undermines the pluralist argument that there is a framework of national interest within which competing groups operate (Knuttila and Kubik 2000). Contrary to the claims of Dahrendorf and others we are more likely confronted by an increasingly complex class system in which inequality remains rife by virtue of the hierarchical power and control structures which ensure restricted access to education, position, status, wealth and income. As Hout et al. (1996) say, class is more complex than Marx envisaged but claims that we are rapidly moving to a classless society are markedly premature. In this context social work is faced with the dilemma of declaring in whose interests it operates if the interests of service users and other groups in society are not consistent with each other in a modern capitalist state.

Post-structuralism and post-modernity – the end of structural thinking?

The many changes witnessed in society in the decades following the Second World War were reflected in a parallel upheaval in theoretical thinking with the recognition of the multiplicity of structures and meanings, and translated into the replacement of structural theorizing with post-structural theorizing from the 1960s. A major consequence was the rejection of objective reality as having meaning and its replacement of reality being defined by subjective experience and its sharing through communication of various forms. In this sense all social reality is constructed by discourse and therefore subject to continual change.

This is in direct contradiction to the claims of set patterns of structure as proposed by theorists such as Marx. Foucault goes as far as to dismiss structural ideas, including those of Marx, as myth and turns his attention to micro-level struggles around identifiable oppressed groups in society whose predicaments are determined by discourses dominated by powerful vested interests (Inglis 2012). For example, the mentally disordered are so because they are given a label defining their condition by those in positions of power, i.e. the psychiatrists. The power of the psychiatrist is derived from their knowledge of mental health which in turn has been constructed by a discourse of these same powerful individuals who control the discourse (Foucault 2006). This is a circular process of creation of meaning by the powerful for the powerful in an attempt to categorize certain others as deviant and present them with a concept of what it is to be normal. The meaning of normality has been constructed in the same way so that the 'psychiatric patient' as an individual becomes trapped in a relatively powerless state. For Foucault this illustrates how knowledge is power and power is knowledge.

Post-structuralism provided the roots for post-modernism which became the preferred terminology from the 1980s on. This reflected the sense of a changing world particularly in terms of social issues and culture across dimensions of gender, sexuality and ability. The primary message from post-modern thinking is that there is no certainty or set order in society based on objectivity or science but rather a kaleidoscope of subjective realities and understandings which results in championing diversity, fluidity and openness in social relations. Post-structuralist and post-modern ideas in rejecting the 'grand' structuralist theories of both the consensus and conflict models whose thinking was based on acceptance of objective, universal reality have highlighted the diversity of relationships in society which an emphasis on subjective experience produces.

The overarching oppression of the proletariat by the bourgeoisie, for example, is replaced by a myriad of oppressions operating between different groups at different times. For Cuff et al. (1998: 255) post-structuralism/modernism means having to challenge oppressions 'at particular points and in fairly specific ways. Poststructuralists have to seek victories at the margins, sometimes through direct political action by particular groups.' The desire for a more equal and just society might remain but the concept of a general revolution led by a mass movement of the oppressed is rejected and replaced by the Foucauldian idea that as power is everywhere then everywhere there is resistance and the potential for this resistance to manifest itself in group reactions (Veyne 2010). This has more recently been referred to as single issue politics which, for Marxists, has dissipated the power which lay in different oppressed groups recognizing their commonalities of class and poverty.

It is immediately possible to see the fit between mainstream social work practice and the post-modern orientation. Recognition and support of diversity and the importance of the individual are core to practice ideas with choice of method often reflecting the preferred eclectic approach. Service users are invariably separated into groups reflecting certain characteristics whether this is age, disability, health condition or behaviour. This delineation influences the design and organization of service delivery into distinct divisions and social workers become employed as specialists in work with one client group or another. Any unity of cause of service users is less discernible as a result and competition for resources between different groups of service users and their social workers becomes the norm of activity. It is also evident that post-modernity has afforded opportunities which have seen the discourse on service users changing to incorporate the language of user involvement and its practice, to a greater or lesser extent in different areas of social service delivery and practice (Wilson et al. 2011).

Complementing this is the emergence of the subjective exercise of reflexivity in the professional tool kit enabling learning to take place from and during interactions with service users (Schön 1983). This is also an intended feature of 'learning organizations' which are a supposed antidote to the managerialism of recent decades with more open, fluid and participative processes and responses (Gould and Baldwin 2004). There have been practical examples of increased campaigning activity by and with people with disabilities, mental health difficulties and children and young people in care. Practice theories have developed such as constructive social work and strengths-based work based on emphasis on service users' subjective narratives. The shift to this post-modern 'micro' approach to social work has, notwithstanding the significance of some of the changes, been eased by the existing platform of the functionalist individualism of traditional mainstream practice. The individual, the subjective and the micro become of an even higher order than previously.

The claims of post-modernism that there is only subjective reality and no such thing as truth do not sit easily with some observers who witness enduring social structures of inequality, power and injustice. It is possible to accept the importance of individual agency in how society operates but this does not have to be at the expense of ignoring macro structural processes. Pierre Bordieu (1977) persuasively demonstrates how it is perhaps less important to argue the counter positions of the micro and the macro, the individual and the collective, than to examine and understand the way in which individual agency is mediated by societal forces so that the two are tied in a relationship of the one influencing the other and vice versa. Through his concept of different forms of capital (economic, social and cultural) he shows how individuals and groups take on the characteristics, expectations and tastes of the class they see themselves belonging to. As Dillon (2010: 422) states the individual does not 'act alone or in some existential vacuum', but rather, 'Individual agency, then, is always constrained, always structured... by formal education, social class, family habits and... cultural codes and practices'. For Bordieu people make choices but within a limited arena determined by an objective class structure through which the unequal distribution of resources makes some choices more likely than others. All the choices we make – what we eat, where we go, our leisure activities, our purchases, our political allegiances – reproduce the existing structural order of status and inequality. Social work is always in danger of ignoring the interplay of agency and structure if not in its language then certainly in its practice. The next chapter will consider methods and approaches in professional social work which offer the potential to redress the mainstream imbalance between the individualistic and the structural through a number of critical and radical approaches. It will look towards forms of practice which work towards realizing the stated professional aspirations of greater social justice and equality.

Key points

1   Mainstream psychology underpins a large proportion of methods used in conventional social work practice with its focus on individual deficits and pathology as the roots of social problems.
2   Much of psychologically based social work practice is aimed at 'fixing' people rather than society.

3   Psychological theories have provided insights which can usefully be incorporated into a knowledge set for social work as a relationship-based activity.
4   Critical psychology recognizes that human thought and action has to be placed in a social context of unequal relationships of power, access to resources, opportunity, wealth and income which give rise to social problems.
5   Sociology directs us to the structures and processes in society which impact on the opportunities, activity and choices people make in their lives.
6   Structural social theories have been superseded by post-modern thinking which in turn has been challenged for failing to recognize the objective reality of large scale inequality and social injustice.
7   The interplay of agency and structure may offer a more effective way of understanding and resolving social problems.
8   Social work will benefit from a practice premised on a model of the interplay of agency and structure in the construction of personal and social problems.

Questions for discussion

1   In what ways do the major perspectives in psychology help or hinder the development of an anti-oppressive social work practice?
2   How might you begin to translate Critical Psychological ideas into methods for practice?
3   Consider the relative merits of structural and post-modern thinking in analysing the construction and resolution of social problems in today's society.

7 Effective critical practice

Social work has a moral obligation to stand up and be accountable for the poor and the disadvantaged in society. It is only by joining together in collective action that the voice of the disenfranchised will be heard and society will change.

(anon 2010)

These are the words of a first year undergraduate social work student taken from an essay on poverty and social work. They are worth holding on to as we work through some of the social work approaches and methods which may contribute to a compilation of that which will best inform a critical and radical way of working with people: a way of working which reflects the interplay between agency and structure without neglecting attention to either. Any such approach should place the achievement of social justice at the centre of social workers' activities and aspirational thinking. As Baines (2007) has argued, there is nothing in life that does not have a political element. All human interaction and endeavour involves power and resources and the struggle for these. Nowhere is the link between agency and structure more succinctly expressed than in the phrase 'the personal is political' (Hanisch 1969). Acknowledging agency within structure allows for the use of aspects of both modernist and post-modern theory and their application in practice. In her critique of anti-oppressive practice Brown (2012: 1) states:

> Blending the strengths of both the modernist foundation of anti-oppressive discourse and of the post-modern critiques of its limitations, allows one to es cape the essentialism and subjectivism of modernist anti-oppressive discourse while emphasising an anti-oppressive agenda that emphasises holding onto a clear political position.

She argues that this will also help practitioners avoid the pitfalls of following dominant discourse in their practice and the lack of position taking afforded by post modernism.

Working individually and collectively to improve the lives of individuals should not be separated out from working to create a socially just world in which such changes can be positively sustained. Without such a connection social work is opened to the accusation that it is changing people to conform to an unjust world which creates a disjunction between what the profession does and what it claims to be about.

Campbell and Baikie (2012: 4) provide a timely reminder of one principle of critical social work: that practitioners strive to 'Achieve congruency among their assumptions, values, theories, concepts, principles and practices'. Complementary to this they warn the practitioner to question the validity of the claims of mainstream social work (see e.g. International Federation of Social Workers' definition of social work: IFSW 2000) to have a commitment to social justice and equality without first analysing its approaches in terms of the congruency they demand from a critical approach.

Critical social work does not imply one method but rather a set of principles for practice based on questioning and analysing society and social service delivery from a position of opposition to that which undermines, disenfranchises, deprives and oppresses people. In previous chapters I have explored the various themes which set the context for understanding the forces in society that produce and maintain injustice, discrimination and oppression and the location of social work within these. By incorporating a critical stance in developing practice, social workers are able to question and analyse these forces and design their interventions around a vision of a world in which the power of these forces is minimized if not removed. Reviewing methods and approaches which have moved away from conventional 'fixing' of people associated with the application of mainstream psychology and biology will help us identify the ingredients of a critical way of working which affords social workers the opportunity to take practical steps to engineer change at a personal, organizational and social level.

Post-modern narrative approaches

In the previous chapter I closed by considering the merits and problems arising from post-modern thinking and ideas so I will begin by reviewing one of the more prominent approaches to arise from post-modernism, that of narrative work or therapy (White and Epston 1990). This is articulated in the development of the direct practice method of constructive social work by Parton and O'Byrne (2000).

In developing their translation of social theory into practice Parton and O'Byrne do not deny the existence of an external constraining reality but do concentrate on the meanings that people put on this as the crucial factor in intervening. Using constructive social work means accepting that we are shaped more by the meanings we put on events than by the events themselves. The aim of constructive practice is to enable people with difficulties to alter, reframe or reconstruct the meanings that they put on external events and situations. Because of the number of possible alternative meanings then it is inevitable that some changes in thinking will be just as unhelpful as those which people start with so the aim is to find new ways of looking at things, not just to revise existing thinking. As Parton and O'Byrne (2000: 173–4) say, 'The way these [alternative constructions] are established is not just by reconstructing and re-storying but by using new constructions and stories to change and reconfigure the world.' The new constructions are expressed as narratives of what is happening from the individual's point of view and these new ways of relating to reality result in behavioural changes consequent on the new way of thinking and talking. This is intended to bring about

improvements in the choices people make and their quality of life through personal agency.

The idea that some constructions are better than others in achieving positive change while being almost self-evident does potentially raise theoretical contradictions as one of the premises of post-modern theory is that no one proposition or viewpoint is of greater value than any other and yet in constructive social work it appears that such evaluations are still necessary as objective judgements have to be made by either the professionals involved or the service user or both. Parton and O'Byrne (2000: 177) attempt to answer this by arguing that constructionism 'aims to demonstrate how we, and others, subjectively construct more and more meaningful ways of objectively understanding who, what and where we are and how this might be otherwise'. One is left having to analyse carefully how the judgement on what constitutes a more meaningful way of understanding is made and who validates this. Ironically another tool of post-modernism, discourse analysis, can be applied here when looking for meanings in the language used to describe this method in practice.

In constructive practice the social worker is no longer an expert but a facilitator of dialogue and conversation through which the service user is able to redefine themself, their problems and the possible solutions. The process of narrative leads to the production of new realities or ways of seeing the world for the service user in collaboration with the professional who brings their own knowledge to the situation but in a relationship of equals. The social worker works with uncertainty and ambiguity which are necessary bi-products of plurality of thinking and knowing. Reality becomes something individual agency manufactures. In a nutshell the stories people tell about their predicament are changed so that the new story enables them to take more personal responsibility and exercise greater choice. Nowhere in this approach is there any explicit reference to addressing the external realities of poverty, inequality, oppression and deprivation as the source of problems and therefore as targets for intervention other than through the mind of the individual service user and possible behavioural changes which accrue. Although objective reality is not denied it is relegated to having little or no meaning outside of the subjective interpretations of individuals. It is difficult to measure the extent to which this takes us beyond conventional practice based in humanistic person-centred approaches even if the theoretical paradigms differ.

It is also interesting to note that the ideas of constructive social work are rooted in concepts employed in family therapy which have been used for three decades or more: reframing the meanings in communications; acting on possibilities for change (i.e. positive feedback loops); resistance to change; and the power of imposed collective beliefs on how we behave and respond (see Carr 2000 for a detailed account of family therapy methods). Constructive social work can help release people to explore their problems as entities separate from them as a person and find alternative ways of thinking and behaviour yet its potential remains ambiguous as, by definition, its outcomes cannot be predicted and to conclude that 'better' or more helpful choices can be made by the individual requires some judgement as described above. In professional intervention this most often involves judgements by both the individual and the professional and these may not always coincide as in protection and mental health work. In constructive social work the service user is the final holder of responsibility for the position they find themselves in. The balance between agency and structure is very much skewed towards the former. Brown (2012) does not believe this has to be the case claiming that it is possible, through blending the modern and the post-modern in narrative therapy, to take a stance against structural forces of oppression while including individual agency and power in the process of change.

Some of the difficulties of narrative work are highlighted in a case example presented by Parton and O'Byrne (2000: 131). In this scenario a mother is considering her own parenting and the move to place her 18-month-old child in permanent alternative care. Analysing the scenario it is possible to see that the social worker enters into free dialogue with the mother but intervenes with statements that clearly direct the conversation. The mother is given considerable scope to talk and reflect giving the impression that she is moving towards finding her own solution to her predicament. The social worker nonetheless makes judgements on the varying quality of the mother's parenting and the risk to the child. When confronted with the mother still wanting to have her child and the shame she will feel at losing her the social worker chooses to attend to the latter issue asking the mother how she thinks she can save face. A successful outcome is considered to be mother being prepared to accept the findings of the 'guardian' appointed to provide a report for the court. It could be argued that the unstated aim of social work intervention has, in this instance, been to get the mother to accept the outcome of losing her child and to acknowledge that this has been a result of her own behaviour and choices. No reference to wider contextual issues such as gender, power, inequality and poverty appear to be required.

This is not to argue that the assessment of risk to the child is anything other than robust and valid but to challenge some of the claims of constructive approaches as empowering and anti-oppressive. The mother is given respect and dignity and the social worker seeks to reduce power differentials between herself and the mother by listening to and encouraging her to explore her interpretations of what is happening. However, the intervention shifts the focus so that the construction of the problem is set within a framework of individualizing, which locates the cause exclusively in the mother's behaviour and choices; she is already vulnerable given her social and economic situation. The micro is emphasized and the macro neglected. The question of practice contributing to the social work aim of social justice is simply not addressed. As Healy (2005: 213) states 'Post [modern] theories promote more critically self-reflective practice by demanding that we interrogate all our assumptions about identity, power and values, yet, in so doing, they also threaten to detract our attention and energies from much-needed broad-scale social change.'

Some 'modernist' approaches

Systems thinking

I have often delivered lectures on systems thinking offering the student and practitioner a framework for practice that tied the individual to the global through a series of interlinked, identifiable structures and influences all operating in such a way as to show the individual's life being contingent on many different external elements at any one time. On the face of it this way of thinking appeared to show that life is a continual interplay between the individual (agency) and their environment (structure) including family, community, school, church, government agencies and other national/international institutions. Although originally drawn from the sciences such as engineering its application to social situations was proposed by Von Bertalanfy (1968), developed for social work practice by authors including Pincus and Minahan (1983) and Goldstein (1973) and promoted as ecological systems thinking in the study of child development and education by Bronfenbrenner (1979). This latter approach was adopted for social work practice by Gitterman and Germain (2008) in their life model of social work practice. Their ecosystems model with the use of eco-maps helps to illustrate the complexity of service users' situations and assists in identifying the need to intervene and produce change at several levels and in a range of systems impacting on the individual.

More recently Eileen Munro (2011b) in her review of child protection has promoted the use of a systems approach to ensure that professionals across all the disciplines involved can more readily learn from the experiences arising from failure to protect. She calls for a move away from focusing solely on the individual case and to learning through a deeper understanding of how the various agencies operate together systemically and what limitations and difficulties this throws up in efforts to safeguard children. Her proposals are yet to be implemented and evaluated.

Much of the theorizing in applied systems thinking, while directing the practitioner to the contextual location of the individual, did little to take work beyond a focus on the individual's negotiation with various agencies and organizations albeit that this would be supported by advocacy roles on the part of the professional. Underlying this was an assumption that with the correct interventions systems could once again work to the benefit of the service user once errors in their function had been corrected. There was a lack of acknowledgement of the possibility of difference of interest or embedded conflict being present in social and structural relationships which renders it essentially functionalist in its theoretical persuasion.

In addition the problems facing people were often seen as just as much a dysfunction in their actions as in other parts of the systemic context. While the choices people make are a factor in any life situation the effects of more macro-level influences tended to be ignored. In practice attempting to bring about change in one agency did not necessarily produce a ripple effect as predicted by the theoretically proposed interconnectedness of different elements. Individual system complexity also has to be taken into account. A service agency might, for example, assess an individual as requiring certain equipment and care support to maintain the person at home but the same agency may be responsible for failing to allocate the required resources to realize meeting the need identified. This in turn is linked to local power differentials and decision-making processes and wider political decisions often based on ideological thinking about issues such a public spending, taxation and the role of the state. Faced with such complexity the individual social worker can be forgiven for focusing on working with the individual in a manageable forum of activity. This inclination will be reinforced by 'specialization' around service user group which affords the social worker the right to claim some matters are outside of their knowledge base and skill set.

Task-centred work

This is a popular method often promoted within social work as moving away from those ways of working deemed to be directed towards 'fixing' and based in principles of empowerment and effectiveness. Doel and Marsh (1992) provide a detailed account of this method. This presents the social worker and service user with the opportunity to negotiate clear outcome goals which the service user can work towards in achievable steps. By building in achievability based on the service user's own assessment of their capacity and ability not only is positive reinforcement inherent in the process but the service user is empowered by being central to the planning and implementation. Partnership is key and respect for the service user as author of their own solutions is central to the success of the approach. The work usually involves drawing up an agreement (often written) to which the social worker and service user are signatories and which specifies the problems to be addressed, the order of priority of problems, the tasks to be undertaken, the goals set to achieve success and the schedule involved. This is designed to enable measurement of achievement, clear evaluation of success and accountability of those involved.

The clarity of this method is no doubt attractive with its measurable, structured and time-limited features which will sit comfortably with current organizational service delivery priorities. For the practitioner it opens the door to a less 'messy' and ill-defined muddling through of the complexity of day-to-day service user predicaments. Potential conflicts between agencies and their professional employees may be tempered by indulgence in a mutually preferred approach particularly if both can claim to be able to achieve measured positive outcomes.

Herein lie some of the shortcomings of this method: arranging work around a contract in a social care setting with an optimistic expectation of success must assume some equivalence between the parties involved. This cannot be guaranteed in many social work situations and it would be difficult to testify to equality of power or control over resources in most instances given the levels of inequality in society and how this manifests itself in the service user's position vis-à-vis the service delivery organization. If the tasks are not successfully accomplished or avoidance or resistance occur then the model will tend to turn attention to the failings of the primary actor, the service user.

The selection of cases for this approach therefore becomes highly significant as so many of social work's usual points of intervention are characterized by deep complexity and enduring severity which require very different thinking in problem construction and resolution. In addition the method fails to address the social, political and economic processes and structures forming the context of people's difficulties (Payne 2005), so further individualizing the process and failing to work towards realizing the social work goal of social justice. Healy (2005) further expresses concerns that the method is too culturally specific and therefore may be unsuitable when working with people who have a less linear understanding of time and may be more inclined to value relationship building and the relating of experiences through narrative.

Strengths and optimism

When Saleebey (2012) sought to introduce a strengths perspective into professional practice it was in reaction to the perceived culture in health and social care which, based on the dominance of psychological analysis, defined people's situations in terms of personal deficit, pathology, abnormality and disorder (Healy 2005). As an alternative the strengths perspective sought to switch attention to service users' abilities and potential to achieve positive change in their lives based on a belief in their innate resilience and desire to be well both psychologically and physically. This meant the focus was to switch from attempting to resolve problems rooted in the past to constructing a goal oriented, future facing way of dealing with difficulties. The worker listens for evidence of strength and resourcefulness rather than deficit and weakness to enable such a process to occur.

The source of the means to do this is found in the service user's own personal resources, strengths and capabilities and built around their vision of what they want to be and how they want things to turn out. As Cree and Myers (2008: 40, original emphasis) say this is not the same as a problem solving approach which 'tends to stress the need for a *worker* to help a service user identify realistic goals and work towards them. The strengths perspective uses service users' hopes and dreams as the way forward, even if they seem to the worker to be unrealistic.' This requires a form of collaborative work in which the professional acts as a facilitator tuning in on the service user's positive aspects and potential and helping them towards a realization of their wishes. Healy (2005) refers to this as the role of a translator helping the service user identify and understand what it is they already possess. By doing this the worker intends to increase the service user's motivation and capacity to achieve positive change. The worker remains open-minded to help ensure that the principles underpinning the approach are not compromised.

This approach clearly has post-modern elements to it. There is the idea of the worker not being an 'expert' and the service user being the architect of their own destiny with the correct support available in a relationship of exchange of ideas about the best way forward. Parker and Bradley (2010) argue that even in situations where the worker is obliged by legal requirements to intervene with a specific mandate the principles of collaboration and exchange can be retained through social workers remaining honest and open with the service user(s). The import given to the view of the service user also indicates a re-affirmation of the relevance of subjective understanding of themselves and their situation. There is a strong sense of self-responsibility and change within the individual as the route to realizing positive outcomes. If the worker can help revitalize the individual or group through subjective change then the message is that energy is then available to take on the environmental obstacles that stand in the way of a better life. Service users will be better placed to develop and use support networks in pursuit of this. Saleebey (2012) stresses the need for membership of a supportive group or community as a necessary condition for achieving desired changes.

A strength-based approach offers the professional a reminder of the importance of addressing interpersonal power differentials through being genuine, acknowledging the value of subjective knowledge and understanding and recognizing the skills and abilities of individuals to tackle hardship. The move away from pathologizing individuals which the approach affords can also be held as a positive. It also suggests the power of collaborative work and the greater potential of collective approaches within communities. It remains unclear as to what is considered to be a strength and who decides this. For example, is the capacity to rise up in protest against an oppressor seen as a strength or is it rather the ability to suffer bravely what life throws at you? That is the question.

In not directing us to the wider macro social forces of organizational, political and economic discrimination and oppression the approach nonetheless fails to call on social workers to challenge policy at these different levels. The responsibility for change appears to be placed at the doorstep of the individual and/or community. There is no reference to the question of why resources in society are not more evenly distributed in the first place and the role this plays in creating social problems and the decreased capacity of the individual and community to achieve change. Healy (2005: 168) makes a further claim that the strengths perspective may not be consistent with some central elements of the social work task in certain situations, particularly the area of statutory interventions in child protection and mental health: 'social workers have a statutory, and an ethical obligation to assess the risk the clients present to themselves or to others. In these contexts, a primary focus on clients' strengths is unviable and may exacerbate some clients' vulnerability to harm themselves or to harm others.'

A bridge to critical practice

The road to critical practice can and has adopted and merged several features of the practice methods reviewed so far. The features identified in the review above which can be carried forward to a construction of effective critical practice include:

1   the acknowledgement of plural realities based on the subjective experiences of different groups and individuals;
2   listening to and giving equal value to people's narratives;
3   the professional social worker as non-expert;
4   switching the professional focus from service users' personal deficit, pathology, abnormality and disorder to their abilities, capacities and potential;
5   de-individualizing people's problems so that the problems can be dealt with separately from the person;
6   the centrality of the service user(s) in the planning, process and implementation of change;
7   the need for partnership between professionals and service users, individually and in community, in producing change;
8   working to minimize power differentials in relationships including that between worker and service user;
9   the need for critical self-reflection on the part of the professional.

As we have seen this acceptance of using elements of modernist and post-modernist thinking and practice is not just supported but promoted by Brown (2012: 1) who makes the case for using the strengths of both modernism and post-modernism while leaving their limitations behind. Her suggested 'blended' approach is aimed at facilitating a more 'critically reflexive anti-oppressive practice'.

The influence of post-modern thinking asserting the plurality of realities has contributed to the emergence of a number of theories and methods of practice and social movements centred on particular groups. Feminist and anti-racist social work are two of the more obvious examples of the former and the latter are exemplified by service users organizing in the areas of physical disability, learning disability, mental health and children in care. In addition to this the tradition of radicalism in social work has seen the development of several approaches over time including Marxist, radical, structural and anti-oppressive practices, all attempting to provide tools for personal and social change within overarching theoretical frameworks. It is to these various approaches that I now turn attention to discover necessary additional ingredients of a critical practice which empowers social workers and service users alike.

Mapping critical practice

Critical social work has evolved from its original adoption of the critical social theory of the 'Frankfurt School' (Campbell and Baikie 2012) and its commitment to not just understand and explain society but to critique and change it. In like manner critical social work seeks to address the impact of an unjust society on people transforming both the society and the way social work operates within it. Different social work approaches have emphasized varying ways in which this can be achieved.

Radical social work

Radical social work provided an alternative to conventional individual casework which had dominated practice in the post-war era up to the 1970s. Individual and social problems under this way of thinking were to be seen as having structural rather than personal causes (Dalrymple and Burke 2006) not least given the rediscovery of poverty (Ferguson and Woodward 2009). Professionalism in social work was also challenged as deleteriously distancing worker from service user (Weinstein 2011). From a Marxist perspective professionalism also steered the social worker away from recognizing their own identity as a worker within the capitalist system. The concept of economic class underpinned the world view adopted by radical workers and this overshadowed any consideration of gender, race or disability. This became an increasing source of tension and discontent among critical thinkers and practitioners in the 1980s and 1990s who felt the focus on class too limiting and insufficient in the face of specific oppressions related to gender, race, disability, etc. (Healy 2005).

In practice radical social work called for workers to come together to take collective action by joining trade unions, to work within their organizations challenging their employers, to form alliances with groups involved in social movements such as tenants' associations and to look to economic and social conditions as the source of people's difficulties rather than blaming the victims (service users). Community and welfare rights work were considered particularly pertinent and could best be complemented by wider political activity. Conventional social work practice was interpreted as a form of social control whereby service users were forced to conform to social arrangements which served the needs of capitalism as opposed to their own. Radical social workers sought to help people to question why they found themselves in states of deprivation and to direct them to the wealthy and powerful in society as the source of their problems. This did not rule out individual casework but required its more oppressive aspects to be discarded (Bailey and Brake 1975) and political action to be considered a necessary ingredient for the achievement of social transformation.

The radical approach's strength is its recognition of the need to tackle the wider sources of people's problems and the commonality of the experience of poverty and deprivation across groups. Having faded from significance in the 1980s there is evidence of a re-emergence of radical practice in social work circles which has adapted to postmodern influences. Ferguson and Woodward (2009) are particularly sympathetic to social workers becoming involved in collective, collaborative, community-based work even if often only small scale and locally based. Bringing people together who share problems and facilitating them to use their agency to create resources, fill gaps and challenge the external sources of their assumed powerlessness is considered extremely empowering. They concede that opportunities for this practice are more readily available in the voluntary service sector as the managerial and purchaser characteristics of state social work still present severe challenges in promoting alternative progressive practices.

Two further means for current expression of radical practice are suggested by Ferguson and Woodward (2009). One is linking up with and learning from service user movements such as those in the areas of mental health and asylum seeking. There are increased opportunities for social work students to experience practice placements in these settings and with the support of their supervisors develop ideas and form networks which they can take with them into their professional practice. A second is learning from and recognizing the overlap of values with the global anti-capitalist movement which is challenging the impact of neo-liberal thinking on people whereby all human life and activity including that of social workers is measured and costed.

These ideas and developments are echoed in the work of Lavalette (2011: 6, original emphasis) who sees little difficulty in integrating community, group and individual work in a new radical social work. He states,

> [S]urely the key element is the *orientation* of the practitioner as they undertake good quality work: whom they involve in work processes and how they communicate and keep service users informed; how they fight for service users' rights and needs and how they locate (and explain) the problems service users and workers face.

Being able to claim to be working with a radical orientation does not necessarily mean you are demonstrating radical practice. Orientation of the worker, while necessary, cannot be the primary outcome by which we measure the presence of radical practice. For example social work students will often say that they have applied anti-oppressive practice. This is usually limited to an account of their inter-personal exchange with a service user with an emphasis on communication skills. It is more difficult to discern how they substantiate the achievement of anti-oppression in terms of clear evidence of service user empowerment or liberation.

A potentially significant manifestation of radical practice today is the formation of the Social Work Action Network (SWAN) in 2006 which Lavalette (2011) sees as running in conjunction with the main trade unions representing social workers. The network is seen as providing practitioners with the opportunity to operate at several levels. These include attending conferences around practice issues, being involved in campaigns to defend different service user groups and social workers and working internationally to defend oppressed people in other countries. It lays claim to a multi-faceted approach challenging the social, economic and political forces of oppression while promoting anti-racist and anti-oppressive practice with an emphasis on service user engagement and participation (Lavalette 2011).

This collective approach is intended to enable individuals to work towards so-cial change in both direct and indirect ways with the sharing of ideas to take back to the workplace, public demonstration, political campaigning and through being a part of a greater voice in representations at organizational, political, state and inter-national/global levels. The emphasis is once again on promoting the collective and rejecting individualized psychologically based interventions.

Structural social work

The potential for social work, in practice, to challenge the mainstream politics that form the legal, organizational and policy frameworks of its activity has long been unrealized according to George et al. (2010). Among the attempts to address this deficit is structural social work. This can be seen as an extension of the radical social work of the 1970s and is founded on an attempt to link people's personal problems with the social processes that disempower them and deprive them of resources. At a theoretical level this approach adopts a critical social theory perspective and through analysing social structures aims to directly confront structural injustices (Healy 2005).

While the focus of radical social work ideas has been on class, structural social work recognizes the diversity of oppressions and in particular the way they interact and reinforce each other in people's lived experiences. Dalrymple and Burke (2006) suggest that diminishing power differentials between professionals and service users is a prime focus of structural work. It involves a combination of using interpersonal communication and working in solidarity with oppressed groups to bring about social change.

Mullaly (1997) acknowledges the contributions of feminist and anti-racist social work and the salience of difference afforded by post-modernism. In doing so he looks forward to the theory base of structural social work growing and developing in the light of learning from the narratives of more oppressed groups and the formation of a 'politics of solidarity'. This disallows a hierarchy of oppressions preferring to seek out the unifying elements that will assist in people working together.

Practising structurally involves several activities based on mutual 'horizontal exchange' relationships as outlined by Mullaly (1997 and 2006), Goldberg Wood and Tully (2006) and others. These include:

- helping people link their individual problems to social processes of oppression such as sexism, racism and disablism – redefining problems in political terms;
- empowerment through working alongside – facilitating oppressed voices to be heard through alliances with service users;
- consciousness raising – reflecting on the effects of social processes and directing change processes at these;
- normalizing problems – helping people see they are not the primary source of their difficulties;
- linking people – bringing together service users with similar experience and problems around unifying issues;
- working within employer organizations to maximize service user receipt of and access to services and resources while working to change the organization to counteract the effects of managerialism, marketization, consumerism and business models in preference for an emphasis on public service;
- external activity – joining social movements, political campaigns and achieving personal consistency of word, thought and behaviour around a world view promoting social justice and equality.

George et al. (2010) provide some live examples of working structurally in mainstream contexts and some of the challenges which need to be addressed and worked with in order to see real improvements and progress in service users realizing their aspirations. Through the use of what they call 'creativity' 'practitioners are able to blend and interconnect micro and macro levels of practice and maintain a focus on political change, while supposedly providing programming and service delivery which is focused only on the individual' (p. 6).

In contradiction to this, Fook (2002) delivers a critique of radical and structural social works derived from her own experiences among other sources. She is concerned by a tendency to positivist certainty about society and people suggested by radical approaches and feels that they do not sufficiently allow for difference and plurality and the nuances and variations of experience revealed in day-to-day social work practice. She has expressed worry that personal agency was in effect denied in a deterministic view of people's predicaments born of an over-simplistic conceptualization of power and identity.

In a reflective preamble to setting out her thoughts on developments in critical practice she identifies one of her core concerns: 'There was an implicit denial of personalised aspects of radical social work, and to me, this also constituted an implicit devaluing of much of social work, in particular women's work within social work' (Fook 1995: 4). This has been addressed, to some extent, in the move to service user inclusion and acknowledgement of the interpersonal in more recent writings on radical and structural practice but those wishing to continue in the profession can still benefit by taking Fook's concerns as a warning to avoid turning critical practice into anti-social work practice.

Feminism and anti-racism in social work

Developments in radical and structural approaches are in no small way indebted to feminist and anti-racist social work. While being quite distinct entities they have highlighted the limiting effects of purely class-based thinking on practice ideas. Healy (2005) refers to the critique of radical social work as gender blind and failing to recognize racial injustice.

Feminist objections remind us that social work is most often done by and practised on women and works across multiple oppressions incorporating gender, race, age, class, ability and sexual orientation (Day and Langan 2007; Dominelli and McLeod 1989; Hanmer and Statham 1999). In her exploration of power, diversity and the interplay of different oppressions Dominelli (2002) addresses concerns that women should not be seen as a homogeneous group while nonetheless being bounded by collective needs and aspirations. She seeks to accept post-modern arguments and combine these with a commitment to collective action for social change. Inherent in her approach is the idea of radical egalitarianism which guides the worker to minimizing power differentials between professional and service user in their interactions.

A feminist perspective in social work means switching the focus of work from seeing practice as allied with the state in keeping women in their place in society and the family, to empowering and liberating women both as service users and practitioners (Dalrymple and Burke 2006). This further enabled issues directly and specifically affecting women and their children, such as domestic and sexual violence and exploitation, to be placed on the agenda for social work attention.

While there are several schools of thought within feminist theory there is a consensus that women's oppression is a structural issue and that a major factor is patriarchy. In adopting the personal as political feminist practice adheres to the idea that individual behaviour reflects and reinforces wider social processes and forces of oppression. This should lead social workers to reflect on the ways in which they have internalized these processes and the impact of this on their work with service users (Healy 2005). This is consistent with the critique in Chapter 6 of mainstream psychological perspectives underpinning social work and looks towards an alternative way of understanding how social inequalities affect service users both individually and emotionally (Hatton 2008).

As most service users experience poverty then most of the women that social workers come into contact with as service users will be poor and poverty is known to disproportionately affect women. This feminization of poverty is referred to by Price and Simpson (2007) in putting the case that there remain high levels of inequality and dependence among women. They draw particular attention to the changing discourse on family with the earlier radical feminist critique of family as a source of women's oppression being replaced by a 'renewed family-based discourse promoted by social work' (p. 86) mainly in response to 'preferred' child care practices. There is a potential tension here which critical social workers need to be attentive to. As Price and Simpson (2007: 87) conclude, 'Despite its rhetoric of "empowerment" social work remains an activity that is concerned with surveillance, and, more importantly, this surveillance often renders structural deficits as personal problems.'

An equal contribution to the development of critical thinking and practice has come from anti-racist understanding. Black people have worked to assert the permeation of racism in society, their common experiences and a commitment to fighting it and building positive images of being black (Dalrymple and Burke 2006). They continue by stating that anti-racism moved social work practice beyond multiculturalism and equality of opportunity to directly challenging unequal power relations at a personal and institutional level.

Healy (2005) talks of anti-racist work being a necessary extension to radical approaches as racial injustice had been neglected in previous class-based analyses of service user predicaments. Dominelli (2008) saw the way in which a predominantly white social work, in helping people to adjust and adapt to their situations, could be seen to be exacerbating, let alone ignoring, forces of racial oppression. This led to her calling for greater recognition and collective challenging of racism while recognizing diversity and personal agency within affected communities.

Powell (2001) asserts that social work has to be prepared to challenge its own historically determined ways of thinking about cultural diversity not least in questioning the dominance of western humanism in its orientation. He argues that anti-racism has to address the concept of multiculturalism so that recognition and celebration of diversity is not used to perpetuate binary divisions such as white/black and the dominance of one over the other, but rather to explore ethnic identity as a continuum through which a greater sense of cultural equality can be achieved and the mentality of colonization dismissed. This is supported in its aim by Dominelli (1994: 33) who states that at the core of anti-racist practice is 'transforming the unequal social relations shaping social interaction between black and white people into egalitarian ones'. Again this is achieved through a combination of actions at a personal, institutional and social level.

Anti-oppressive practice

Dalrymple and Burke (2000: 14) have offered a summary definition of anti-oppressive practice (AOP) as 'A radical social work approach which is informed by humanistic and social justice values and takes account of the experiences and views of oppressed people. It is based on an understanding of how the concepts of power, oppression and inequality determine personal and structural relations.' Essential to achieving this are working in partnership, minimal intervention and critical reflection and reflexivity (Dalrymple and Burke 2006). Incorporating humanism as a value base into the definition immediately conflicts with Powell's (2001) warning that this could undermine achieving cultural egalitarianism. However, Dominelli (2002) similarly claims adherence to a person-centred philosophy in anti-oppressive practice. This epitomizes the tension between structure and agency: the individual and the collective which AOP sets out to resolve in offering a framework for practice.

Healy (2005) summarizes the five principles of anti-oppressive practice: critical reflection of self in practice; critical assessment of service users' experiences of oppression; empowering service users; working in partnership; and minimal intervention. The last of these should not necessarily conflict with the need for social workers to act to protect individuals, using the law as required. The worker has to understand the way in which their own personal biography in relation to social divisions affects their working relationships with service users. This has to be allied with a knowledge and understanding of the roots and causes of various oppressions and their maintenance by dominant discourses which permeate government and organizational policy and theories and methods of practice. Equipped with these the professional is in a position to work in an empowering way using strengths-based approaches and awareness raising with service users while addressing service delivery issues at an organizational level. Healy (2005) distinguishes it from earlier critical practice approaches on the grounds that it acknowledges the aggregating role of small local changes in achieving social change. Political campaigning to reform political, social and economic structures for more just distribution of resources and power in society is a further strand to be applied. With these elements in place the relationship with the service user should appear as one of partnership.

Hines (2012) gives an example of applying anti-oppressive practice in working with lesbians. She promotes a proactive practice to assert lesbian identity through openly challenging received ways of thinking in the individual, families and wider society. This moves the worker from individual work to collective approaches including the use of groupwork to reframe thinking on lesbianism and assist in confronting oppressive behaviour. Practitioners are asked to join together with each other and with service users and not remain isolated in their efforts to bring about change.

AOP attempts to afford overarching principles of practice which recognizes the many forms of oppression manifested in power differentials present in social divisions, which themselves characterize relationships between worker and service user. This requires professionals to continually reflect on their actions so as to avoid reproducing oppressive interpersonal and social relations even in situations where managing risk challenges the service user's personal decision making. Recognizing different social divisions and how they operate conforms to post-modern modes of thinking but has the potential to divert attention from the commonalities of oppressive experience if the worker does not apply the intellectual sophistication required. This contributes to the argument for critical thinking to be firmly embedded in social work training curricula where the ability of students in this sphere has been found wanting (Heron 2006).

Brown (1994) notes that there is increasingly less attention given to what people have in common with more to difference and plurality. She observes that 'too singular a focus on competing forms of oppression threatens divisiveness, resulting in the fragmentation and subsequent immobilisation of joint forces for social action' (Brown 2012: 1). The extent to which critical reflection in practice and seeking

social change work in parallel or are integrated in a blended approach is one measure by which AOP can be judged as to how far it reaches beyond the individual and
the interpersonal.

There will be many ways of doing AOP but the critical aspect lies in looking
outwards from the individual and asking 'who is the problem a problem for?' (Fook
2002: 19) and then seeking the solution in collective partnership. If, however, the focus
is on multiple single issues we are nonetheless left with a rather disparate picture of
activity with little sight of overall social change. As Brown (2012) has warned above
collective action around a single issue can serve to undermine collective action around
identified common forces of oppression in society. If AOP enters the mainstream of
social work and concentrates on self-awareness and personal reflection then the cause
of social justice is not furthered and is possibly hindered. Anti-oppression is too readily
adopted by governments, organizations and policy makers transforming their own
identities from sources of oppression to champions of the downtrodden (McLaughlin
2005). Critical workers, using AOP, will turn the gaze of their critique on the sources
of social injustice and the propensity for AOP to be re-balanced in this direction.

One way in which AOP can be self-reflective and re-balanced is through always
being open to alternative discourses supplied by those who sit outside of the normal
forums of power and control. Although post-modernists critique standpoint theory
for ignoring diversity of viewpoint (Brown 2012), Wilson and Beresford (2000: 567)
contest that 'Standpoint theory would hold that service users who find themselves on
the receiving end ... are better placed to generate critical questions and knowledge
claims about ... their oppression'. Developing this I would contend that this is not the
same as listening to the service user's voice and including them in decision making and
other processes because they are seen as experts. It is also about service users having
an impact from the outside pursuing what they believe to be in their interests through
whatever means they have available, whether or not their viewpoint is any nearer the
truth than that of anyone else.

It is about people involved in power struggles and the challenge to the professional is where and with whom to locate themselves in these struggles. Despite an
allegiance to subjectivity, diversity and difference acting anti-oppressively also require
position taking. This is a real and enduring contradiction in which a clear world view
and commitment to social justice have to sit with being open to critical reflection at
all times. However, without the former there is little direction and with only the latter
there is endless analysis and inertia. Effective practice will encompass the operation
of reflection within unambiguous stated values which define political and ideological
boundaries. This would minimize any tendency to superficially assert that oppressions
are automatically reproduced in, for example, a white male working with a black female and at the same time allow for the identification of actions which perpetuate
inequality, deprivation and discrimination. Dorling (2012: 346) offers some simple advice: 'What works in one place does not often work in other places, but if you have
a rough idea of where you are trying to get to, and you try most of the time to make
steps towards that, you won't go too far wrong.'

Bell (2012) articulates what she calls a post-conventional paradigm for social work
in which individual knowledge is seen as always shared, exchanged and transformed

through constant interrelations within situations such as poverty. She sees this as an alternative to the objectivity of positivism and an 'antedote' to the individualism of relativity. She claims that, 'Seeking service users' knowledge in this way ensures that *epistemic agency is* afforded to social work clients as participants' (p. 419, original emphasis). This suggested commonality of social service and service user aims through incorporation may not be immediately evident to the latter and a working through of what divides social work from service user might first be needed.

It may be that it is in the milieu of power struggles that discourses are made more transparent, awareness thrives, individual narrative is reframed and personal and collective agency reinforced. The lived experience of being in struggle or conflict provides the platform for expressing one's position politically in the pursuit of social justice and helps turn the 'idea' of anti-oppression into actuality. As Bell (2012: 414) confirms we should 'acknowledge the broader context from which knowledge originates as well as its broader social implications'.

A critical practice will negate any belief that AOP is achieved through only professional reflexivity and attempts at equalization of power in interpersonal social work interventions. The social worker has to see beyond this for fear of developing the delusion that they operate AOP in a context of anti-oppressive service delivery. The consideration of power in organizations in Chapter 4 gives a stark reminder of the constraints that context can impose on the professional's ability to employ problem free anti-oppressive practice. Sinclair and Albert (2008: 5) remind us of the threat that anti-oppressive practice could, in reality, become 'mostly an intellectual activity relegated to the abstract realms of theory as opposed to a personal, political and practical activity where individual involvement is not absolved'.

Closing thoughts on critical practice

The binding thread through the debate so far has been the tension between personal agency and the influence of structure. This is underpinned by the difficult to reconcile theoretical positions proffered by post-modernism on the one hand and modernism on the other. I have discussed several forms of practice which have sought to combine the two through blending, creativity, soft or subtle reality and integrative methods. In exploring the literature it becomes clear that there is an acknowledgment of the validity and importance of post-modern concepts in affirming diversity, identity, difference, subjective reality and the value of service user knowledge and agency. However, there remains a concern that the meaning and nature of social work needs redefining theoretically so that workers are liberated to properly pursue all the elements of a critical practice which is truly anti-oppressive and addresses social issues of poverty, deprivation and inequality. Trevithick (2012) catalogues the limitation of a number of social work methods in neglecting the social causes of problems and the political dimension in perpetuating them.

Such is the resilience of established ways of service delivery that some social workers deem alternatives as beyond their scope. In discussing critical practice in a lecture recently one student humorously declared, 'Excuse me while I put on my

Wonderwoman outfit and fly off to sort out society between visits to service users'. This exemplifies the way in which the pursuit of social justice and collective work are seen as separate from the role of a social worker. The dominance of evidence-based practice tends to support this separation as the methods drawn from this are largely psychologically based or set within a medical model (Herz 2011). The idea that there can be 'proof' of what works and that outcomes will be similar for all people partaking in intervention programmes is core to this way of thinking at the same time as being highly positivistic and individualistic.

One criticism of current social work is that the individualism of modernist, conventional approaches has been replaced by the individualism of cultural relativity and identity with the consequent neglect of the pursuit of social change or reconstruction so vital to the pursuit of social justice and equality (Houston 2001). Bell's (2012) post-conventional paradigm moves us closer to seeing individual agency as interconnected through relationships and therefore that is should never be considered or dealt with in isolation offering greater potential for collective responses. Her writing does not take us much beyond meaningful service user participation based on independent representation but it does open the door to more depth in thinking about the nature, cause and resolution of people's problems.

A promising alternative third way is proposed by critical reality theory which challenges the relativism embedded in social constructionism while maintaining that the individual can actively change the world around them at the same time as being changed by it (Bhaskar 1998). For the critical realist the social world is made up of many open systems, including causal mechanisms, some of which are subjective (e.g. the service user and their experience) and others which are objective (e.g. the economic system). The significance lies in the fact that these multiple systems, not all of which are immediately observable, are in a permanent state of interaction, forever altering each other and so are never fixed and deterministic as in strict structural explanations. Herz (2011: 4) represents the connectedness of the subjective (service user experience), the relational (interaction with others), the positional (class, gender, ethnicity, etc.) and the structural (institutions of government, law, economy, etc.) in a linear, two-way flow chart demonstrating that social work interventions need understanding and action at different levels. Critical reality would reconstruct this as a more fluid, less predictable moving set of systems which collide and interact with less certainty.

We arrive in a world where humankind operates agency with structure rather than agency within structure, representing a more complex interactional relationship and promoting a more positive orientation towards social change. Service user knowledge remains valued and valid, not as expert knowledge but as vulnerable and tentative and weaved from its interaction with other mechanisms. In similar fashion social work and social workers are part of the same dynamic. Seeking to change one mechanism outside of its interlocution with others is rendered redundant (Houston 2001). As Houston suggests, helping someone suffering unemployment by facilitating a change in their personal narrative without attacking the other causal mechanisms of unemployment would be considered facile. The intellectual skills of social workers are of primary import in critical reality as working anti-oppressively within this theoretical framework requires them 'to think systemically, deductively and critically if they are to probe deeply into case material' (Houston 2001: 856). I would suggest that this might give preference to the use of collective methods working at the multifaceted intersections of systems to more deeply understand and change causal processes.

Herz (2011) specifically suggests participation in regular group conferences and seminar style discussions and refers to the development of 'research circles' in Swedish municipalities as a useful model to adopt. The explosion in IT, global communication and social networking affords much greater opportunities in this sphere for the imaginative worker. Group work and other social action oriented activity with the aim of raising consciousness and eradicating human misery are also brought more to the foreground. Mantle and Backwith (2010) put the case for community oriented social work (COSW) as an effective poverty aware approach to social change. Central to COSW is social work's direct involvement in local communities through political campaigning, advocacy and community organization including preventive strategies such as engaging with credit unions and helping form supportive collectives of community members. Partnership can be made a reality by knowing the community through profiling, being seen to be organizing for change within employer organizations and openly challenging political decisions and policies. Acting collectively at all times will protect against individual professional sacrifice where social workers are accountable to both employers and service users.

Being apolitical is not an option as Mantle and Backwith (2010: 13) state: 'social workers should not attempt to play "neutral" because in so doing, they allow the status quo to continue unchallenged'. The need for a social work force with a clear identity committed to critical anti-oppressive activity consistent with the stated aim of achieving social justice and greater equality is as strong today as ever. There is a persistent force in the shape of 'an influential neoliberal agenda that transforms social problems at the structural and collective level to problems relating to individual performance and behaviour' (Herz 2011: 6). If social work fails to see this and acquiesces in this dynamic process which is well underway then its own agency will have made a significant contribution to its own demise. Social work continues to state its commitment to human rights, social justice and fairness but more importantly these words must be translated into actions which show the profession is true to its word.

Key points

1   All of life is political and social work is not exempt from this.
2   Critical social work is a set of principles for practice based on questioning and analysing society and social service delivery from a position of opposition to that which undermines, disenfranchises, deprives and oppresses people.
3   Critical social work seeks to address the impact of an unjust society on people transforming both the society and the way social work operates within it.
4   Bringing together elements of both modernist and post-modernist thinking secures the best route to effective critical practice.
5   All approaches and methods in social work have strengths and weaknesses. The critical thinker is able to analyse these using a clear world view and commitment to social justice.

6   The potential for social work, in practice, to challenge the mainstream politics that form the legal, organizational and policy frameworks of its activity has too long been unrealized.

7   Linking the personal, organizational and social is essential to an understanding of and effective response to the causal processes of oppression.

8   Recognition of different oppressions does not preclude organizing around common experiences which unite people.

9   Employing collective methods in social work is an almost wholly neglected yet essential feature of effective critical practice. These include groupwork with service users, conferencing, seminars, research circles, community orientation and involvement, political campaigning, electronic communication and social networking.

10   If social work does not resist current directions in social and political policy it is in danger of becoming one of the authors of its own destruction.

Questions for discussion

1   What do you consider to be the key features of an effective critical practice?

2   What changes would you target in your organization to empower social workers and facilitate critical practice?

3   Can the modern and the post-modern be reconciled to offer a meaningful challenge to individualizing tendencies in social work?

Bibliography

Alcock, P. (2006) *Understanding Poverty*, 3rd edn. Basingstoke: Palgrave Macmillan.

Alibhai-Brown, Y. (2010) Yes. Get rid of this oppressive symbol, *New Humanist*, 125(5): 26–7.

Althusser, L. (1977) *Lenin and Philosophy and Other Essays*. London: Verso.

Backwith, D. and Mantle, G. (2009) Inequalities in health and community-orientated social work: lessons from Cuba? *International Social Work*, 52(4): 499–511.

Bailey, R. and Brake, M. (eds) (1975) *Radical Social Work*. London: Edward Arnold.

Baines, D. (ed.) (2007) *Doing Anti-oppressive Practice: Building Transformation Politicized Social Work*. Winnipeg: Fernwood.

Baldwin, M. (2011) Resisting the EasyCare model: building a more radical, community based, anti-authoritarian social work for the future, in M. Lavalette (ed.) *Radical Social Work Today*. Bristol: Policy Press.

Banks, S. (2006) *Ethics and Values in Social Work*, 3rd edn. Basingstoke: Palgrave Macmillan.

Barker, P. and Davidson, B. (1997) *Psychiatric Nursing: Ethical Strife*. London: Hodder Arnold.

Barney, D. and Dalton, L. (2006) Social work under Nazism: an analysis of the profession-in-the-Environment, *Journal of Progressive Human Services*, 17(2): 43–62.

BASW (2011) *Code of Ethics*. BASW College of Social Work.

Bauman, Z. (1993) *Postmodern Ethics*. Oxford: Wiley-Blackwell.

BBC (2012) Councils refer record number of children into care. *News UK*, 9 January, http://www.bbc.co.uk/news/uk-16958373 (accessed 17 July 2012).

Becker, S. (1997) *Responding to Poverty*. Harlow: Longman.

Beckett, C. and Maynard, A. (2011) What are values, in V.E. Cree (ed.) *Social Work: A Reader*. Abingdon: Routledge.

Bell, K. (2012) Towards a post-conventional philosophical base for social work, *British Journal of Social Work*, 42(3): 108–23.

Bell, V. (2002) *Debates in Psychology*. Abingdon: Routledge.

Bentham, J. (1948) Introduction, *The Principles of Morals and Legislation*. New York: Hafner.

Beresford, P. (2011) Radical social work and service users: a crucial connection, in M. Lavalette (ed.) *Radical Social Work Today*. Bristol: Policy Press.

Beresford, P. and Croft, S. (2004) Service users and practitioners re-united; the key component for social work reform, *British Journal of Social Work*, 34: 53–68.

Bhaskar, R (1998) General introduction. in M. Archer, R. Bhaskar, A. Collier, T. Lawson and A. Norrie (eds) *Critical Realism*. Abingdon: Routledge.

Biestek, F.P. (1961) *The Casework Relationship*. London: Allen & Unwin.

Blok, W. (2012) *Core Social Work: International Theory, Values and Practice*. London: Jessica Kingsley.

Bourdieu, P. (1977) Cultural reproduction and social reproduction, in J. Karabel and A.H. Halsey (eds) *Power and Ideology in Education*. Buckingham: Open University Press.

Brandon, M., Bailey, S. and Belderson, P. et al. (2009) *Understanding Serious Case Reviews and their Impact. A Biennial Analysis of Serious Case Reviews 2005–2007. Research Report: DCSF-RR129*. London: Dept for Children, Schools and Families.

Brandsen, T. (1998) De manager als modern held. [The manager as a modern hero]. *Tijdschrift voor de Sociale Sector*, 9(52): 4–7.

Brechin, A., Brown, H. and Eby, M.A. (eds) (2000) *Critical Practice in Health and Social Care*. London: Sage/Open University.

Brewer, M., Browne, J. and Joyce, R. (2011) *Child and Working Age Poverty and Inequality in UK: 2010. IFS Commentary C121*. London: Institute for Fiscal Studies.

Bronfenbrenner, U. (1979) *The Ecology of Human Development: Experiments by Nature and Design*. Cambridge, MA: Harvard University Press.

Brown, C.G. (1994) Feminist postmodernism and the challenge of diversity, in A. Chambon and A. Irving (eds) *Essays on Postmodernism and Social Work*. Toronto: Canadian Scholar's Press.

Brown, C.G. (2012) Anti-oppression through a postmodern lens: dismantling the master's conceptual tools in discursive social work practice, *Critical Social Work*, 13(1).

Brown, K. and Rutter, L. (2008) *Critical Thinking for Social Work*, 2nd edn. Exeter: Learning Matters.

Burke, P. and Parker, J. (2007) *Social Work and Disadvantage*. London: Jessica Kingsley.

Burman, E. (1994) *Deconstructing Developmental Psychology*. Hove: Routledge.

Burman, E. (ed.) (1998) *Deconstructing Feminist Psychology*. London: Sage.

Burrell, G. and Morgan, G. (1979) *Sociological Paradigms and Organisational Analysis: Elements of the Sociology of Corporate Life*. London: Heinemann.

CAFCASS (2012) *Care Demand Statistics*. http://www.cafcass.gov.uk/publications/care_demand_statistics.aspx

Callinicos, A. (1999) *Social Theory: A Historical Introduction*. Cambridge: Polity Press.

Campbell, C. and Baikie, G. (2012) Beginning at the beginning: an exploration of critical social work, *Critical Social Work*, 13(1).

Carr, A. (2000) *Family Therapy: Concepts, Process and Practice*. Chichester: Wiley.

Cemlyn, S. (2008) Human rights practice: possibilities and pitfalls for developing emancipatory social work, *Ethics and Social Welfare*, 2(3): 222–42.

Child Poverty Action Group (2011) Poverty Watch, *Poverty*, 139(Summer): 20.

Chung, C.M. and Hyland, M.E. (2012) *History and Philosophy of Psychology*. Chichester: Wiley-Blackwell.

Clark, C.L. (2000) *Social Work Ethics: Politics, Principles and Practice*. Basingstoke: Macmillan.

Clifford, D. and Burke, B. (2009) *Anti-oppressive Ethics and Values in Social Work*. Basingstoke: Palgrave Macmillan.

Cohen, G.A. (2008) *Rescuing Justice and Equality*. Cambridge, MA: Harvard University Press.

Collins, S. (2009) Some critical perspectives on social work and collectives, *British Journal of Social Work*, 39(2): 334–52.

Coughlan, S. (2011) UK seeing 'a big rise in poverty' says ISF. http://www.bbc.co.uk/news/education-15242103 (accessed 17 July 2012).

Cree, V. and Myers, S. (2008) *Social Work: Making a Difference*. Bristol: The Policy Press.

Cross, S., Hubbard, A. and Munro, E. (2010) Reclaiming Social Work: London Borough of Hackney Children and Young People's Services. London: Borough of Hackney.

Cuff, E.C., Sharrock, W.W. and Francis, D.W. (1998) *Perspectives in Sociology*. Abingdon: Routledge.

Cunningham, J. and Cunningham, S. (2008) *Sociology and Social Work*. Exeter: Learning Matters.

Dahrendorf, R. (1959) *Class and Class Conflict in an Industrial Society*. London: Routledge.

Dalrymple, J. and Burke, B. (2000) Anti-oppressive practice, in M. Davies (ed.) *The Blackwell Encyclopaedia of Social Work*. Oxford: Blackwell.

Dalrymple, J. and Burke, B. (2006) *Anti-oppressive Practice: Social Care and the Law*. Maidenhead: McGraw-Hill.

Davey, I. (1977) Radical social work: what does it mean in practice? *Social Work Today*, 8(23): 8–10.

Davies, R. (1968) The Lyre of Orpheus, cited in Calhoun, C. (1996) Social theory and the public sphere, in B.S. Turner (ed.) *The Blackwell Companion to Social Theory*. Oxford: Blackwell.

Davis, A. and Wainwright, S. (2005) Combating poverty and social exclusion: implications for social work education, *SW Education*, 24(3): 259–73.

Day, L. and Langan, M. (2007) *Women, Oppression and Social Work: Issues in Antidiscriminatory Practice*. Kindle edition. Abingdon: Taylor and Francis.

Deacon, A. (2004) Different interpretations of agency within welfare debates, *Social Policy and Society*, 3(4): 447–56.

Deetz, S. (1996) Describing difference in approaches to organisation science: rethinking Burrell and Morgan and their legacy, *Organisation Science*, 7(2): 191–207.

DeNavas-Walt, C., Proctor, B.D. and Smith, J.C. (2011) *Income, Poverty and Health Insurance Cover in the United States: 2010. US Census Bureau, Current Population Reports, P60-239*. Washington, DC: US Government Printing Office.

Department for Education and Skills (2006) *Care Matters: Transforming the Lives of Children and Young People in Care*, CM6932. Norwich: HMSO.

DfCLG (2011) *Fire Kills Campaign: Annual Report 2011*. London: Department for Communities and Local Government.

Dillon, M. (2010) *Introduction to Sociological Theory*. Chichester: Wiley.

Doel, M. and Marsh, P. (1992) *Task-centred Social Work*. Farnham: Ashgate.

Dominelli, L. (1994) Anti-racist perspectives in the social work curriculum, in L. Dominelli, N. Patel and W.T. Bernard. *Anti-racist Social Work Education: Models of Practice*. SSSU.

Dominelli, L. (2002) *Feminist Social Work: Theory and Practice*. Basingstoke: Palgrave.

Dominelli, L. (2008) *Anti-racist Social Work*, 3rd edn. Basingstoke: Palgrave Macmillan.

Dominelli, L. (2010) Anti-oppressive practice, in M. Gray and S.A. Webb (eds) *Ethics and Value Perspectives in Social Work*. Basingstoke: Palgrave Macmillan.

Dominelli, L. and McLeod, E. (1989) *Feminist Social Work*. Basingstoke: Macmillan.

Dorling, D. (2012) *Fair Play: A Daniel Dorling Reader on Social Justice*. Bristol: Policy Press.

Drakeford, M. and Gregory, L. (2008) Anti-poverty practice and the changing world of credit unions: new tools for social workers, *Practice*, 20(3): 141–50.

Drydakk, N. (2010) Religious affiliation and employment bias in the labour market, *Journal for the Scientific Study of Religion*, 49(3): 477–93.

Dubois, B. and Miley, K. (2005) *Social Work: An Empowering Profession*. Boston, MA: Pearson.

Ehrenreich, B. (2010) *Nickel and Dimed*. Cambridge: Granta Books.

Elks, S. (2012) *Family cuts forcing our youth into dire straits, Metro Newspaper*, 10 January.

Elliott, L. and Aitkenhead, D. (2012) It's payback time: don't expect sympathy – Lagarde to Greeks, *Guardian*, 25 May.

End Child Poverty (2012) *Child Poverty Map of the UK*. End Child Poverty, hosted by Child Poverty Action Group, London.

End Child Poverty (2012) Why End Child Poverty: The Effects. http://endchildpoverty. org.uk/why-end-child-poverty/poverty-in-your-area (accessed 17 July 2012).

Ferguson, I. and Lavalette, M. (2004) Beyond power discourse: alienation and social work, *British Journal of Social Work*, 34: 297–312.

Ferguson, I. and Woodward, R. (2009) *Radical Social Work in Practice*. Bristol: Policy Press.

Fook, J. (1995) Social work: asking the relevant questions. Paper presented at the 24th National AASW Conference, Launceston. Tasmania.

Fook, J. (2002) *Social Work: Critical Theory and Practice*. London: Sage.

Foucault, M. (2001) *Dits et Ecrits*. Paris: Gallimard.

Foucault, M. (2006) *Psychiatric Power*. Basingstoke: Palgrave MacMillan.

Fournier, V. (1999) The appeal to 'professionalism' as a disciplinary mechanism, *The Sociological Review*, 47(2): 280–307.

Fox, D. and Prilleltensky, I. (eds) (1997) *Critical Psychology: An Introduction*. London: Sage.

French, J. and Raven, B.H. (1959) The bases of social power, in D. Cartwright (ed.) *Studies in Social Power*. Institute for Social Research.

Fukuyama, F. (1992) *The End of History and The Last Man*. London: Penguin.

Gans, H.J. (1971a) Poverty and culture: some basic questions about methods of studying lifestyles of the poor, in P. Townsend (ed.) *The Concept of Poverty*. London: Heinemann.

Gans, H.J. (1971b) The uses of poverty: the poor pay all, *Social Policy*, July/August: 20–4.

George, P., Coleman, B. and Barnoff, L. (2010) Stories from the field: practicing structural social work in current times: practitioners' use of creativity, *Critical Social Work*, 11(2). http://www.unwindsor.ca/criticalsocialwork/stories-from-the-field-practicing-structural-socialwork-in-current-times-practitioners%E2%80%99-use-of-crea.

George, V. and Howards, I. (1991) *Poverty Amidst Affluence: Britain and the United States*. Cheltenham: Edward Elgar.

Giddens, A. (1984) *The Constitution of Society*. Cambridge: Polity.

Giddens, A. (1997) *The Consequences of Modernity*. Cambridge: Polity.

Gilbert, T. and Powell, J.L. (2010) Power and social work in the United Kingdom: a Foucauldian excursion, *Journal of Social Work*, 10(1) January, pp. 3–22.

Gilligan, P. (2007) Well motivated reformists or nascent radicals: how do applicants to the degree in social work see social problems, their origins and solutions, *British Journal of Social Work*, 37(4): 735–60.

Gitterman, A. and Germain, C. (2008) *The Life Model of Social Work Practice: Advances in Theory and Practice*, 3rd edn. New York: Columbia University Press.

Goldberg Wood, G. and Tully, C.T. (2006) *The Structural Approach to Direct Practice in Social Work: A Social Constructionist Perspective*, 3rd edn. New York: Columbia University Press.

Goldstein, H. (1973) *Social Work Practice: A Unitary Approach*. Columbia: University of South Carolina Press.

Goodman, A. and Gregg, P. (2010) *Poorer Children's Educational Attainments: How Important are Attitudes and Behaviour?* York: Joseph Rowntree Foundation.

Goodman, S. and Trowler, I. (eds) (2011) *Social Work Reclaimed*. London: Jessica Kingsley.

Gough, B. and McFadden, M. (2001) *Critical Social Psychology: An Introduction*. Basingstoke: Palgrave.

Gould, N.G. and Baldwin, M. (2004) *Social Work, Critical Reflection and the Learning Organisation*. Farnham: Ashgate.

Gramsci, A. (1971) *Selections from the Prison Notebooks*, edited and translated by Quintin Hoare and Geoffrey Nowell Smith. London: Lawrence and Wishart.

Gray, M. and Webb, S.A. (2010) *Ethics and Value Perspectives in Social Work*. Basingstoke: Palgrave Macmillan.

GSCC (2010) *Codes of Practice for Social Care Workers*. London: General Social Care Council.

Habermas, J. (1992) *Moral Consciousness and Communicative Action*. Cambridge: Polity.

Hacker-Wright, J. (2009) Human nature, personhood and ethical naturalism, *Philosophy*, 84(329): 413–27.

Hanisch, C. (1969) *The Personal is Political*. Gainesville Women's Liberation.

Hanmer, J. and Statham, D. (1999) *Women and Social Work: Towards a Woman Centred Practice*, 2nd edn. Basingstoke: Palgrave Macmillan.

Hatton, K. (2008) *New Directions in Social Work Practice*. Exeter: Learning Matters.

Hayes, N. (2002) *Psychology in Perspective*, 2nd edn. Basingstoke: Palgrave.

Healy, K. (2000) *Social Work Practices: Contemporary Perspectives on Change*. London: Sage.

Healy, K. (2005) *Social Work Theories in Context: Creating Frameworks for Practice*. Basingstoke: Palgrave.

Healy, K. (2012) *Social Work Methods and Skills: The Essential Foundations of Practice*. Basingstoke: Palgrave Macmillan.

Healy, K. and Meagher, G. (2004) The reprofessionalisation of social work: collaborative approaches for achieving professional recognition, in L. Davies and P. Leonard (eds) *Social Work in a Corporate Era: Practices of Power and Resistance*. Farnham: Ashgate.

Hearn, J. (2012) *Theorizing Power*. Basingstoke: Palgrave Macmillan.

Heath, P. (1997) Translation, 'I Kant, Lectures on Ethics'. Cambridge: Cambridge University Press.

Heron, G. (2006) Critical thinking in social care and social work: searching students' assignments for the evidence, *Social Work Education*, 25(3): 209–24.

Herz, M. (2011) Critical social work – considerations and suggestions, *Critical Social Work*, 12(1).

Hines, J.M. (2012) Using an anti-oppressive framework in social work practice with lesbians, *Journal of Gay and Lesbian Social Services*, 24(1): 23–39.

Hobbes, T. (2008) *Leviathan*, Edited by J.C.A. Gaskin. Oxford: Oxford Paperbacks.

Hobbes, T. (2010) The natural condition of mankind. in P. Schumaker (ed.) *The Political Theory Reader*. Chichester: Wiley Blackwell.

Holton, R.J. (1997) Classical social theory, in B.S. Turner (ed.) *The Blackwell Companion to Social Theory*. Oxford: Blackwell.

Hooper, C.A., Gorin, S., Cabral, C. and Dyson, C. (2007) *Living with Hardship 24/7: The Diverse Experiences of Families in Poverty in England*. London: Frant Buttle Trust.

Houston, S. (2001) Beyond social constructionism: critical realism and social work, *British Journal of Social Work*, 31(6): 845–61.

Houston, S. (2010) Discourse ethics, in M. Grey and S.A. Webb (eds) *Ethics and Value Perspectives in Social Work*. Basingstoke: Palgrave Macmillan.

Hout, M., Brooks, C. and Manza, J. (1996) The persistence of classes in post-industrial society, in D.J. Lee and B.S. Turner (eds) *Conflicts About Class: Debating Inequality in Late Industrialism*. London: Longman.

Howe, D. (1987) *An Introduction to Social Work Theory*. Aldershot: Ashgate.

Howe, D. (1992) *An Introduction to Social Work Theory*, 3rd edn. London: Wildwood House.

Howe, D. (2009) *A Brief Introduction to Social Work Theory*. Basingstoke: Palgrave Macmillan.

Howe, D., Brandon, M., Hinings, D. and Schofield, G. (1999) *Attachment Theory, Child Maltreatment and Family Support*. London: Macmillan.

Hugman, R. (1991) *Power in Caring Professions*. London: Macmillan.

Hugman, R. (2011) An ethical perspective on social work, in V.E. Cree (ed.) *Social Work: A Reader*. Abingdon: Routledge.

IASSW (2001) *International Definition of Social Work*. Hong Kong: IASSW.

Ife, J. (1997) *Rethinking Social Work: Towards Critical Practice*. London: Longman.

IFSW (International Federation of Social Work) (2000) Definition of social work at http://www.ifsw.org/f38000138.html (accessed 17 July 2012).

Ingleby, E. (2006) *Applied Psychology for Social Work*. Exeter: Learning Matters.

Inglis, D. (2012) *An Invitation to Social Theory*. Cambridge: Polity.

Irvin, G. (2008) *Super Rich: The Rise of Inequality in Britain and the United States*. Cambridge: Polity.

Johnson, S. and Moorhead, B. (2011) Social eugenics practices with children in Hitler's Nazi Germany and the role of social work: lessons for current practice, *Journal of Social Work Values and Ethics*, 8(1).

Jones, C. (1998) Poverty, in M. Davies (ed.) *The Blackwell Companion to Social Work*. Oxford: Blackwell.

Jones, C. (2001) Voices from the front line: state social workers and New Labour, *British Journal of Social Work*, 31(4): 547–62.

Jones, C. (2002) Poverty and social exclusion, in M. Davies (ed.) *The Blackwell Companion to Social Work*, 2nd edn. Chichester: Wiley-Blackwell.

Jones, C. (2011) The best and worst of times: reflections on the impact of radicalism on British social work education in the 1970s, in M. Lavalette (ed.) *Radical Social Work Today*. Bristol: Policy Press.

Jones, C. and Novak, T. (1999) *Poverty, Welfare and the Disciplinary State*. London: Routledge.

Joseph, J. (2006) *Marxism and Social Theory*. Basingstoke: Palgrave Macmillan.

Kazdin, A.E. (1975) *Behaviour Modification*. Homewood, IL: Irwin.

Killeen, D. (2008) *Is Poverty in the UK a Denial of People's Human Rights?* York: Joseph Rowntree.

Knuttila, M. and Kubik, W. (2000) *State Theories*, 3rd edn. London: Zed Books.

Kuhn, T.S. ([1962] 1996) *The Structure of Scientific Revolutions*, 3rd edn. Chicago: Chicago University Press.

Lavalette, M. (ed.) (2011) *Radical Social Work Today*. Bristol: Policy Press.

Lewis, O. (1961) *The Children of Sanchez*. London: Penguin.

Lister, R. (2004) *Poverty*. Bristol: Polity.

Locke, J. (2010) The second treatise of government, in P. Schumaker (ed.) *The Political Theory Reader*. Chichester: Wiley Blackwell.

Lukacs, G. (1971) *History and Class Consciousness*. London: Merlin.

Lukes, S. (2005) *Power: A Radical View*, 2nd edn. Basingstoke: Palgrave Macmillan.

McLaughlin, K. (2005) From ridicule to institutionalisation: anti-oppression, the state and social work, *Critical Social Policy*, 25: 283–305.

McMahon, W. (2006) The politics of anti-social behaviour, *Safer Society*, 28, Spring.

Malik, S. (2012) Sick and disabled people could be forced to work for nothing, *Guardian*, 17 February.

Malim, T. and Birch, A. (1998) *Introductory Psychology*. Basingstoke: Palgrave Macmillan.

Mantle, G. and Backwith, D. (2010) Poverty and social work, *British Journal of Social Work*, 40(8): 2380–97.

Marmot, M. (2010) *Fair Society, Healthy Lives: Strategic Review of Health Inequalities in England Post-2010*, The Marmot Review.

Martin, K. and Hart, R. (2011) Trying to get by: children and young people talk about poverty, *Poverty*, 139: Summer.

Maslow, A.H. (1965) Self-actualisation and beyond. Address to the Conference on The Training of Counsellors of Adults, Chatham, Massachusetts, 22–28 May.

Maslow, A.H. (2011) *Toward a Psychology of Being*. Radford: Wilder Publications.

Miliband, R. (1977) *Marxism and Politics*. Oxford: Oxford University Press.

Mills, C.W. (1951) *White Collar*. Oxford: Oxford University Press.

Milton, J., Polmear, C. and Fabricius, J. (2011) *A Short Introduction to Psychoanalysis*, 2nd edn. London: Sage.

Mitchell, F., Neuburger, J., Radebe, D. and Rayne, A. (2004) Living in limbo: survey of homeless households living in temporary accommodation, *Shelter*, June: 24–5.

Monnickendam, M., Katz, Ch. and Monnickendam, M.S. (2010) Social workers serving poor clients: perception of poverty and service policy, *British Journal of Social Work*, 40(3): 911–27.

Morss, J.R. (2002) *Growing Critical: Alternatives to Developmental Psychology*. London: Routledge.

Mullaly, B. (1997) *Structural Social Work: Ideology, Theory and Practice*. Oxford: Oxford University Press.

Mullaly, B. (2006) *The New Structural Social Work: Ideology, Theory and Practice*. Oxford: Oxford University Press.

Munro, E. (2011b) *The Munro Review of Child Protection. Interim Report: The Child's Journey*. London: Department for Education.

Munro, E. (2011a) *The Munro Review of Child Protection. Final Report: A Child Centred System*. London: Department for Education.

Myers, J.C. (2010) *The Politics of Equality*. London: Zed Books.

Narayan, D., Patel, R., Schafft, K., Rademacher, A. and Koch-Schulte, S. (2000) *Voices of the Poor: Can Anyone Hear Us?* Oxford: Oxford University Press.

Novak, T. (1984) *Poverty and Social Security*. London: Pluto.

Nozick, R. (2001) *Anarchy, State and Utopial*. Chichester: Wiley-Blackwell.

Orton, M. (2009) Understanding the exercise of agency within structural inequality: the case of personal debt, *Social Policy and Society*, 8(4): 487–98.

Outhwaite, W. (2009) *Habermas*, 2nd edn. Cambridge: Polity.

Parker, J. and Bradley, G. (2010) *Social Work Practice*, 3rd edn. Exeter: Learning Matters.

Parsons, T. (1969) *Politics and Social Structure*. New York: Free Press.

Parton, N. (2008) Changes in the form of knowledge in social work: from the 'social' to the 'informational'? *British Journal of Social Work*, 38: 253–69.

Parton, N. and O'Byrne, P. (2000) *Constructive Social Work: Towards a New Practice*. Basingstoke: Palgrave Macmillan.

Paylor, I. and Washington, J. (2000) Social exclusion and inequalities in the United Kingdom, *Critical Social Work*, 1(2).

Payne, M. (2005) *Modern Social Work Theory*, 3rd edn. Basingstoke: Palgrave Macmillan.

Payne, M. (2006) *What is Professional Social Work?* Bristol: BASW/Policy Press.

Pemberton, C. (2010a) Courts to make own assessments of child asylum seekers' age. www.communitycare.co.uk (accessed 17 July 2012).

Pemberton, C. (2010b) Social workers 'need more input' in tackling child poverty. www.communitycare.co.uk (accessed 17 July 2012).

People First Lambeth (2010) An urgent letter to the Government, *Shaping Our Lives. National User Network Newsletter*, 23 November, p. 10.

Pincus, A. and Minahan, A. (1983) *Social Work Practice: Model and Method*. Illinois: F.E. Peacock.

Poulantzas, N. (1976) The capitalist state: a reply to Miliband and Laclau, *New Left Review*, 95: January–February.

Poulter, J. (2005) Integrating theory and practice: a new heuristic paradigm for social work practice, *Australian Social Work*, 58(2): 199–212.

Powell, F. (2001) *The Politics of Social Work*. London: Sage.

Price, D. (2006) The poverty of older people in the UK, *Journal of Social Work Practice*, 20(3): 251–66.

Price, V. and Simpson, G. (2007) *Transforming Society? Social Work and Sociology*. Bristol: Policy Press.

Radcliffe, N. and Timimi, S. (2005) The rise and rise of attention deficit hyperactivity disorder, *Journal of Public Mental Health*, 4(2): 9–13.

Ramesh, R. (2012) Cuts in children's services risk greater inequality, says expert, *Guardian*, 15 February.

Rawls, J. (2005) *A Theory of Justice*. Cambridge, MA: Harvard University Press.

Rix, J. (2011) A breakaway success, *Guardian*, Society, 9 November.

Roberts, I. (1995) Deaths of children in house fires: fanning the flames of child health advocacy? *British Medical Journal*, 311(7017): 1381–2.

Robinson, L. (2009) *Psychology for Social Workers: Black Perspectives on Human Development and Behaviour*, 2nd edn. Abingdon: Routledge.

Rogers, C.R. (2003) *Client Centred Therapy: Its Current Practice, Implications and Theory*. London: Constable.

Rogers, C.R. (2004) *On Becoming a Person*. London: Constable.

Rokeach, M. (1973) *The Nature of Human Values*. New York: Free Press.

Rorty, A. (2010) Questioning moral theories. *Philosophy*, 85(331): 29–46.

Rose, N. (1999) *Powers of Freedom: Reframing Political Thought*. Cambridge: Cambridge University Press.

Saleebey, D. (2011) Power in the people, in V.E. Cree (ed.) *Social Work: A Reader*. Abingdon: Routledge.

Saleebey, D. (2012) *The Strengths Perspective in Social Work Practice*, 6th edn. Boston:Pearson.

Scheyett, A. (2006) Silence and surveillance: mental illness, evidence-based practice, and a Foucauldian lens, *Journal of Progressive Human Sciences*, 17(1): 71–92.

Schön, D. (1983) *The Reflective Practitioner: How Professionals Think in Action*. New York: Basic Books.

Searing, H. (2011) Barefoot Social Worker. www.radical.org.uk/barefoot/ (accessed 17 July 2012).

Shardlow, S. (2009) Values, ethics and social work, in R. Adams et al. (eds) *Social Work: Themes, Issues and Critical Debates*, 3rd edn. Basingstoke: Palgrave Macmillan.

Sheldon, B. (1982) *Behaviour Modification*. Abingdon: Routledge.

Sheldon, B. (1995) *Cognitive-behavioural Therapy: Research and Practice in Health and Social Care*, 2nd rev. edn. London: Routledge.

Shelter (2009) *Shelter's Response to the Marmot Review Consultation: Health Inequalities in England Post-2010*. Shelter.

Sinclair, R. and Albert, J. (2008) Social work and the anti-oppressive stance: does the emperor really have new clothes, *Critical Social Work*, 9(1).

Skinner, B.F. (1991) *The Behaviour of Organisms*. New York: Appleton Century Crofts.

Smith, P. (2008a) *Moral and Political Philosophy*. Basingstoke: Palgrave Macmillan.

Smith, R. (2008b) *Social Work and Power*. Basingstoke: Palgrave Macmillan.

Soydan, H. (1999) *The History of Ideas in Social Work*. London: Venture Press.

Spicker, P. (2007) *The Idea of Poverty*. Bristol: Policy Press.

Stepney, P. (2006) Mission impossible? Critical practice in social work, *British Journal of Social Work*, 36(8): 1289–307.

Steyaert, J. and Gould, N. (2011) Social work and the changing face of the digital divide, in V.E. Cree (ed.) *Social Work: A Reader*. Abingdon: Routledge.

Strier, R. and Binyamin, S. (2009) Developing anti-oppressive services for the poor: a theoretical and organisational rationale, *British Journal of Social Work*, 40(6): 1908–26.

Tavris, C. and Wade, C. (1995) *Psychology in Perspective*. London: HarperCollins.

Taylor, C. (1967) *The Explanation of Behaviour*, 3rd edn. London: Routledge and Kegan Paul.

Terry, L. (2007) Ethics and contemporary challenges in health and social care, in A. Leathard and S. McLaren (eds) *Ethics: Contemporary Challenges in Health and Social Care*. Bristol: Policy Press.

Thompson, N. (2005) *Understanding Social Work: Preparing for Practice*. Basingstoke: Palgrave Macmillan.

Thompson, N. (2006) *Power and Empowerment (Theory into Practice)*. Lyme Regis: Russel House.

Timimi, S. (2005a) ADHD: the medicalisation of naughty boys, *Human Givens*, 12: 10–15.

Timimi, S. (2005b) *Naughty Boys: Anti-social Behaviour, ADHD and the Role of Culture*. Basingstoke: Palgrave Macmillan.

Timimi, S. and Taylor, E. (2004) ADHD is best understood as a cultural construct, *British Journal of Psychiatry*, 184(1): 8–9.

Trevithick, P. (2012) *Social Work Skills and Knowledge: A Practice Handbook*. Maidenhead: Open University Press.

Umbarger, C.C. (1983) *Structural Family Therapy*. New York: Grune and Stratton.

US GPO (1965) Lyndon B. Johnson's special message to Congress, 16 March 1964. *Public Papers* of *U.S. Presidents, Lyndon B. Johnson, 1963–1964, 1, 375–380*. Washington: Government Printing Office.

Veyne, P. (2010) *Foucault: His Thought, His Character*. Cambridge: Polity.

Von Bertalanfy, L. (1968) *General Systems Theory: Foundations, Development, Applications*. New York: George Braziller.

Vornanen, R., Hämäläinen, J. and Pölkki, P. (2011) Influences of the economic recession and hardship on child welfare policy and practice in Finland, *Dialogue in Praxis*, 13(21): 7–22.

Wachtel, H. (1972) Capitalism and poverty in America: paradox or contradiction, *American Economic Review*, 62(2): 187–94.

Waiton, S. (2006) Antisocial behaviour: the construction of a crime. www.spiked-online.com/index.php?/site/article/5/ (accessed 17 July 2012).

Webb, S.A. (2010) Virtue ethics, in M. Gray and S.A. Webb (eds) *Ethics and Value Perspectives in Social Work*. Basingstoke: Palgrave Macmillan.

Weber, M. (1992) *Economy and Society*. Berkeley, CA: University of California Press.

Weber, M. (2009) *Max Weber: A Biography*. Piscataway, NJ: Transaction Publishers.

Weinstein, J. (2011) Case con and radical social work in the 1970s: the impatient revolutionaries, in M. Lavalette (ed.) *Radical Social Work Today*. Bristol: Policy Press.

White, M. and Epston, D. (1990) *Narrative Means to Therapeutic Ends*. London: W W Norton & Co.

Whittington, C. and Whittington, M. (2007) Ethics and social care: political, organisational and interagency dimensions, in A. Leathard and S. McLaren (eds) *Ethics: Contemporary Challenges in Health and Social Care*. Bristol: Policy Press.

Wilding, P. (1982) *Professional Power and Social Welfare*. Abingdon: Routledge.

Wilkinson, S. (ed.) (1996) *Feminist Psychologies: International Perspectives*. Buckingham: Open University Press.

Wilson, A. and Beresford, P. (2000) Anti-oppressive practice: emancipation or appropriation? *British Journal of Social Work*: 30(5): 553–73.

Wilson, K., Ruch, G., Lymbery, M. and Cooper, A. (2011) *Social Work. An Introduction to Contemporary Practice*, 2nd edn. Boston, MA: Pearson Education.

Wood, G.G. and Tully, C.T. (2006) *The Structural Approach to Direct Practice in Social Work*, 3rd edn. New York: Columbia University Press.

Index

SOCIAL WORK POCKETBOOKS

Assessments
in Social Work
with Adults

Elaine Aspinwall-Roberts

In association with
COMMUNITYcare

ASSESSMENTS IN SOCIAL WORK WITH ADULTS

Elaine Aspinwall-Roberts

9780335245215 (Paperback)
May 2012

eBook also available

This accessible survival guide shows social workers how to make their assessments the best, most effective and person-centred they can be.

Part of a new Social Work Pocketbooks series, the book is friendly, non-patronising and realistic about the day-to-day difficulties and challenges associated with assessing adults. It encourages you to reflect on how you work, and what you bring to the task.

Key features:

- Practical examples, advice and tips, including dealing with pitfalls
- Good practice and point of law reminders
- Fresh ideas on how to develop your assessment skills with adults

www.openup.co.uk

SOCIAL WORK POCKETBOOKS

Report Writing

Daisy Bogg

REPORT WRITING

Daisy Bogg

9780335245130 (Paperback)
May 2012

eBook also available

Report writing is a key social work skill, and one in which many practitioners receive very little formal training and preparation.

Part of a new Social Work Pocketbooks series published in association with Community Care, this easy to use guide will assist you in producing professional, informative and good quality reports. It provides key information, hints and tips to help you to develop your report writing style and to consider best practice in your written communication.

Key features:

- A range of report templates
- Examples of good practice in report writing
- Specialist chapters covering legal, policy and assessment situations

www.openup.co.uk

SOCIAL WORK POCKETBOOKS

Applying a
Personalised
Approach to
Eligibility Criteria

Daisy Bogg

In association with
COMMUNITYcare

**APPLYING A PERSONALISED APPROACH
TO ELIGIBILITY CRITERIA**

Daisy Bogg

9780335245154 (Paperback)
2012

eBook also available

The eligibility criteria for social care services can be difficult to apply to complex needs. Part of a new **Social Work Pocketbooks** series, this book includes a range of useful practice suggestions and guidance to help social workers think about how they can apply eligibility to psychosocial issues and needs to ensure individuals are able to access appropriate support options.

Key features:

- Describes the legal frameworks
- Realistic case study examples
- Practice suggestions and checklists

www.openup.co.uk

OPEN UNIVERSITY PRESS
McGraw - Hill Education

Working with Substance Users

Kim Heanue and Chris Lawton

9780335245192 (Paperback)
2012

eBook also available

This book, part of the Pocketbook series, will be a useful tool not only for experienced professionals but also newly qualified social workers and students. It deals with topics such as why people take substances and the risks involved as well as suggesting ways to deal with challenging situations.

Key features:

- A practical desk guide for social workers to refer to on a day-to-day basis.

www.openup.co.uk

SUPERVISION

Bill McKitterick

9780335245253 (Paperback)
October 2012

eBook also available

Supervision has a special place in the development of social work practice skills and continuing professional development. However it can be neglected or overshadowed. Part of a new **Social Work Pocketbooks** series, this book focuses on the practical and workable ways for preparing for and using supervision, ensuring it is provided and making improvements if it is not working for you.

Key features:

- Practical ways for both the supervisor and social worker to prepare for and use supervision
- Strategies to improve supervision or get it started again when it has fallen into disuse
- Realistic examples of good and bad practice

www.openup.co.uk